THE STORY OF
MOHAMMED

DISCOVERY PUBLISHER

2015, Discovery Publisher

Author : Edith Holland
Editor : Adriano Lucca

DISCOVERY PUBLISHER

dp

616 Corporate Way
Valley Cottage, New York, 10989
www.discoverypublisher.com
books@discoverypublisher.com
facebook.com/DiscoveryPublisher
twitter.com/DiscoveryPB

New York • Tokyo • Paris • Hong Kong

TABLE OF CONTENTS

Forewords 11

Yussouf 12

Arabia and Its Tribes 14

The Year of the Elephant 19

The Youth of Mohammed 26

Mohammed as a Prophet 33

The Year of Mourning 41

The Pledge of Al-Akabah 48

The Flight from Meccah 57

The City of the Prophet 63

Mohammed as a Lawgiver 70

The Day of Deliverance 76

The Field of Uhud 84

The Siege of Medinah 89

The Pledge of the Tree 96

The Taking of Meccah 104

The Submission of Taif 111

The Farewell Pilgrimage 118

THE STORY OF
MOHAMMED

ASIA MINOR
TURKEY
Erzerum
Euphrates

PIAN SEA
Balfrush
Astrabad

KA
KA
PUN.
IND
SIND

Herat
AFGHANISTAN
Kabul

Kelat
BALUCHISTAN

KHORASAN

PERSIA

Yezman
KURISTAN
Bender Abbas

Tabriz
Teheran
IRAK
Ispahan
Ispahan

Shiraz

Aleppo
Hamah
Homs
Damascus
Bostra
Jerusalem
PALESTINE
Baghdad
Tigris
IRAK
MESOPOTAMIA
Euphrates

Persian Gulf
EL HASA
Basra

G. of Oman
Maskat
Ras el Hadd
OMAN

SYRIAN
DESERT
HAMAD
NEFUD DESERT

ARABIA

Al-Akabah
Al-Hijr
Tabuk

Khaibar
Mt Uhud
Al-Madinah

KASIM
Shaggera
EL Koffut
NEJD
YEMAMA

SANDY DESERT OF ROBA-EL-KHALI
OR DAHNA

HADRAMAUT
Tarim
Maiblaf
JAUF
NEJRAN
Sheba

HIJAZ
Dhat-irk
Mt Arafat
Taif
Meccah
Badr

Sadwan
ASIR

YEMEN

RED SEA

Suez
Suez
EGYPT
Alexandria
TERRANEAN
SEA
Cyprus

Suakin
Massowah
ERITREA

Khartum

ARABIAN
SEA
Bor

Kuria Muria Is.

English Miles
0   100   200   300   400   500

Forewords

A FEW YEARS AFTER St. Augustine landed on the Isle of Thanet to preach Christianity to the people of Britain, Mohammed, the Prophet of Arabia, began to preach against the idolatry of his native land, exhorting his country-men to the worship of the True God. He met with much opposition, but succeeded in the end in overthrowing idolatry and establishing the faith of Islam throughout the greater part of Arabia. The wandering tribes of the desert, united by the ties of a common faith, became a great nation, and spread themselves over many of the countries of Asia and Northern Africa. They even crossed the Straits of Gibraltar and founded a kingdom in Spain. During several hundred years the followers of Mohammed were the chief promoters of art, science, and literature. More than once a Mohammedan race threatened to overrun Europe, an event which would have changed the whole course of history; it was about a thousand years before such a possibility disappeared. At the present day many millions of the inhabitants of India, Persia, Afghanistan, Turkey, Egypt, and various parts of Africa are Moslems, or followers of the Prophet Mohammed; it is but right that we should know something of the founder of so wide-spread a faith, and of the beliefs professed by so many of our fellow-men.

Yussouf

A stranger came one night to Yussouf's tent,
Saying, "Behold one outcast and in dread,
Against whose life the bow of power is bent,
Who flies, and hath not where to lay his head;
I come to thee for shelter and for food,
To Yussouf, called through all our tribes the Good."

"This tent is mine," said Yussouf, "but no more
Than it is God's; come in, and be at peace;
Freely shalt thou partake of all my store,
As I of His who buildeth over these
Our tents his glorious roof of night and day,
And at whose door none ever yet heard Nay."

So Yussouf entertained his guest that night,
And, waking him ere day, said: "Here is gold;
My swiftest horse is saddled for thy flight;
Depart before the prying day grows bold."
As one lamp lights another, nor grows less,
So nobleness enkindled nobleness.

That inward light the stranger's face made grand
Which shines from all self-conquest.
Kneeling low, He bowed his forehead upon Yussouf's hand,
Sobbing, "O Sheik, I cannot leave thee so;
I will repay thee; all this thou host done
Unto that Ibrahim who slew thy son!"

"Take thrice the gold," said Yussouf, "for with thee
Into the desert, never to return,
My one black thought shall ride away from me.
First-born, for whom by day and night I yearn,
Balanced and just are all of God's decrees;
Thou art avenged, my first-born, sleep in peace!"

J. R. LOWELL

Arabia and Its Tribes

If you look at the map of Asia you will find, in the southwest, the largest peninsula in the world. This is Arabia; its shape is an irregular oblong, bounded on the west by the Red Sea, on the south by the Indian Ocean, on the east by the Persian Gulf and the river Euphrates, and on the north by Syria.

Arabia is a very hot and dry country; in some parts it scarcely ever rains, and a great deal of it is desert. Except in the southwest, there are no rivers that flow the whole year round, they rush in torrents from the mountains in springtime, but soon lose themselves in the sand, leaving dry river-beds, which are called wadys. The Arabs are a very ancient people, having possessed their land from the earliest days of which we have any records, and they have never been wholly conquered by any foreign invader.

The Arab nation is divided into tribes; in olden days there was no king or ruler over the whole of Arabia, but each tribe was independent, and governed by its chief. This chief was usually chosen because he was the bravest or the wisest man, and the one best fitted to lead. Some of the tribes lived in towns and villages and had settled occupations, whilst others were Bedouins, or wanderers, and lived in tents, moving their camps from place to place when they wanted fresh pasture for their flocks and herds. In their wanderings they often had to cross wide tracts of desert, and their most useful beast of burden was the camel. No animal is better fitted for travelling in the desert than the camel; he is very hardy and able to go without water for several days together, and his feet, being large and flat, are specially adapted for walking on the soft sand. The camel has been well named the ship of the desert.

Have you any idea what a desert is like? Imagine a land from which all life has disappeared—where there are no hedges, nor trees and flowers; no birds, no insects. The hills are barren, the valleys dry beds of forgotten rivers; there is no sound nor sign of life—a world of nothingness! Think how far away the horizon appears when you stand on the beach, looking out to sea; if you were in the desert this far horizon would be round you on all sides, smoky blue in the dim distance, and you would feel lost in the boundless expanse.

In some parts of the desert there are sand dunes—hillocks and mounds of sand as soft as down cushions, blown by the wind into ridges that are like the waves of the sea. Sometimes the wind blows fiercely across the open waste, and the loose sand rises up like a tall pillar and overspreads the sky, blotting out the sun. Any camels that may be on the march lie down and bury their noses in the sand, and their riders lie beside them, covering up their mouths and noses until the sandstorm has swept by. Can you wonder that the people who live on the borders of the great desert should think of Paradise as a garden with flowing rivers?

The Arabs are the children of the desert, and many of their special qualities can be traced to its influence. What people have a greater love of freedom than the wandering Arabs who roam over these vast solitudes, knowing no limit or boundary, for the desert is free to all? The wiry strength and endurance of the Arab, his quickness of perception, are the outcome of his desert life, for to the wayfarer of the sandy waste "voyaging is victory," and he must use all his resourcefulness, all his powers of endurance, to defeat the dangers that beset him on his way. Perhaps it is these pitiless regions which have inspired the fierce revengefulness of the Arab, for he is slow to forgive an injury, and a blood feud may sometimes last for generations. On the other hand, no people in the world are so famed for their hospitality as these wanderers of the desert. The weary traveller need never appeal in vain for food and shelter; his Arab host will entertain him with the best he has, often killing his last sheep or goat to do honour to his guest. So highly does an Arab regard the duty of hospitality that if a stranger has once broken bread or eaten salt with him he considers him ever afterward entitled to his protection, even though he should turn out to be his worst enemy.

Three men were once having a discussion as to who was the most generous of all the Arabs they knew. Each claimed that distinction for his own particular friend, quoting instances of his wonderful liberality. The discussion became heated, and at length some one suggested that each of the three men should go to his friend, asking for help, and the one who responded most liberally to the appeal would be considered the first among the Arabs for generosity. This was agreed to, and the first man went in search of his friend, Abdallah, whom he found mounted on his camel, and just about to start on a journey. But when Abdallah heard that his friend was travelling and in need of help he immediately dismounted and told him to take the camel and all that was on her; the only thing he asked to have back was a sword he greatly valued, which hung on the saddle. The saddle-bags on the camel were found to contain four thousand pieces of gold and some silk vests, but the most valuable article was the sword.

The second of the two men now went to test the generosity of his friend, whose name was Kais. When he arrived at his house Kais was asleep, and his slave did not like to wake him, but hearing that a friend of his master was in need of help he gave him all the money he could find in the house, amounting to several thousand pieces of gold, and told him to go to the man in charge of the camels and take a camel and a slave. When Kais awoke he commended his servant for what he had done, and, as a reward, gave him his freedom, but said that if he had seen his friend himself he would have given him still more.

It now remained for the third man to try if his friend Arabah could surpass the other two in acts of generosity. Arabah was infirm and nearly blind; he was on his way to prayers, leaning on the arms of two slaves, when he met his friend, who appealed to him for help. "Alas! I have no money," cried Arabah, deeply distressed, "but take these slaves, for they are all I have." His friend refused, but Arabah insisted, and, dismissing his two slaves, he groped his way as best he could along the walls of the houses.

When the three men met to discuss the merits of their friends, all who were present were of the same opinion—that Arabah had proved himself the most generous, for he had given all he possessed.

There were three things on which the ancient Arabs specially prided themselves—eloquence, with a thorough knowledge of their own beautiful language, horsemanship, including the use of arms, and the practice of hospitality. Without these no Arab was considered to be fully educated.

The Arabs have a great love of poetry. In the olden days their only historical records were contained in the verses of their poets. So highly did they value this art that when a new poet arose, his tribe was publicly congratulated. A festival was held in his honour, and the women danced and sang to the sound of timbrels. Only two other occasions were considered worthy of public rejoicing that of the birth of a son and of a purebred Arab foal, for the Arabs are very proud of their breed of horses, which are famous all the world over.

At the great fairs, which were held yearly at certain places in Arabia, poetical competitions used to take place. The poets came and recited their verses before all the people, and those which were judged to be the best were written on silk in letters of gold and hung up in the ancient temple of Mecca, where all might see them. It may seem strange to you that this wild and lawless people should have had such a passion for poetry; but the free and wandering life of the desert is more likely to foster the true spirit of poetry than the atmosphere of civilized towns. When guarding his flocks from the wild beasts that infest the borders of the desert, the Arab would often spend his nights under the "stars which are the poetry of heaven"—shining in those clear skies with a brilliancy we have no idea of in our misty northern climes. The cold light of dawn, touching the summits of the grey hills, giving them a grim and haggard look, the mirage shimmering in the noon-day heat, the crimson sunset lighting the rocks with a, radiance like the glow of a fiery furnace—these airings lent wings to the imagination of the lonely watcher, and quickened his insight into the world of mystery and romance. Was not one of the greatest poets of all time an Arab for the *Book of Job* contains some of the finest poetry that was ever written?

There is yet another side to the teaching of the desert; in the loneliness of this vast and empty land, man realizes his helpless dependence, and his faith in a merciful and compassionate God who cares for his needs, becomes stronger and more vivid. It was in the desert that Abraham, journeying by the guidance of the stars, came to the knowledge of an all-powerful God, far above the vain idols of man's imaginings. Moses, during his long sojourn in the wilderness, never doubted the near presence of a mighty God, a sure help in time of trouble. In later years the Prophet of Arabia, wandering among the barren hills of his native land, saw in the wonders of nature sure signs of the greatness of the Creator, and there came upon him the conviction that "God is One, the Eternal," that "there is none like unto Him." In the desolation of the desert man looks to a Paradise in the unknown land beyond the stars—there will he find a haven of rest, a heavenly city, "gardens neath which rivers flow."

The desert is an all-conquering force which man has no power to overcome, and where it seeks to extend its boundaries its advance is irresistible. The sand, lashed by the cutting winds, is for ever driven against the solid rocks; gradually their outline is effaced, until, in the long course of ages, they too crumble away into particles of sand. The work of destruction never ceases. Step by step the desolation advances, spreading over all a veil of sand, like a mantle of forgetfulness.

The Year of the Elephant

On the western side of Arabia, in the province of Hijaz, and about fifty miles from the Red Sea coast, is the city of Meccah. It is one of the oldest cities in the world and one of the most interesting. As long ago as the days of Jacob it was an important centre for the caravans bringing their rich merchandise from the south, and through the desert into Syria. You read in the Psalms, "The kings of Arabia and Saba shall bring gifts." Saba was a city on the southwest coast of Arabia, in the province of Yemen, which is much more fertile than other parts of the country. In the olden days there must have been many stately towns along that coast, and it was from this part of Arabia that the Queen of Sheba came to visit Solomon.

Gold and precious stones and many sweet-smelling spices were brought to Yemen from the shores of Africa, and even from India. All this valuable merchandise was loaded on the backs of camels to be conveyed to the markets of Syria and other important centres of trade, sometimes even to Egypt and the ports of the Mediterranean. The merchants travelled in companies or caravans, for the sake of safety, for there were many dangers to be faced before they could reach the end of their journey. A great part of the route lay through the desert, and here were often plunderers who might fall on the caravans, robbing them of all their treasures. A caravan may be large or small, a large one sometimes numbering over a thousand camels.

At certain places in the desert there are fertile spots called oases. A spring of water coming to the surface causes grass and palm-trees to grow, and the latter are much prized and carefully cultivated for the sake of their dates. A well is usually built to prevent the precious spring from being choked up with sand. An oasis may consist of a single well and a few palms, or it may be very large, containing thousands of date palms and villages with many inhabitants. At these fruitful islands the caravans halted, while the weary travellers enjoyed a well-earned rest and replenished their store of water, which they carried in goatskin bags. On the road from Yemen to Syria there are about seventy halting-places, Meccah lying about half-way.

The sacred city of Meccah is situated in a long, narrow valley, almost entirely surrounded by steep mountains, on which there is hardly a trace of vegetation. There are no green fields to be seen, and this spot, so reverenced by the Arabs and all Mohammedans, is one of the most grim and barren places of the earth. There are many legends connected with its early history. It is said that, after their wanderings in the wilderness, Hagar and Ishmael came into the valley of Meccah; Hagar, unable to find water for her son, left him lying on the ground, and ran distractedly between the hills of Safa and Marwah, seeking a well or a spring. When she returned to her child there was a stream of clear water gushing from the ground at his feet! This spring was afterward known as Zem-Zem, the sacred well which is to this day visited by pilgrims. Near this spot the city of Meccah was founded; in course of time Ishmael married the daughter of one of the ruling chiefs, and he is reverenced as the forefather of many of the tribes of Arabia.

In the midst of the city stands a very ancient temple. Its shape is that of a perfectly plain four-sided figure, the height being rather greater than the length and breadth; the sides of the building are entirely covered with a drapery, usually of black. The Kaabah, or Cube House, as this temple is called, is regarded by the Mohammedans as the most sacred place on earth. It is in no way beautiful, yet its severe simplicity makes it one of the most impressive sights in the world. At the southeast corner of the building, near the only door, is inserted a mysterious Black Stone, which has been held in reverence by countless generations. A legend tells that it once fell from heaven, and was originally white, until the sins of the world changed it to its present colour. Very little is known about the early history of the Kaabah. The Arabs say that the first Kaabah was built by the angels for Adam in Paradise, and that the earthly Kaabah was an exact copy of this first model. It was many times destroyed, and was supposed to have been rebuilt by the Patriarch Abraham with the help of his son Ishmael. The Arabs say that it was Abraham who first taught them the worship of the true God and instituted some of the ceremonies of pilgrimage to the Holy House.

For a time the Arab tribes followed the religion of Abraham, but by degrees they fell away from their ancient faith and became idolaters. At the time at which our story begins, the whole of Arabia was given over to idolatry. Some of the tribes worshipped the stars and planets, the beautiful Sirius, or Dog Star, being an object of special devotion; some made idols of stones and rocks, and a few were fire-worshippers, like the early Persians. Thus the Kaabah, which had first been devoted to the service of God, became a shrine of idolatry. In the sixth century there were 360 idols, one for each day of the Arab year, around and within the Kaabah. These idols were of various forms, one being in the shape of an eagle, another of a horse, and among them stood a rude statue of the Patriarch Abraham. One of the most honoured was Hubal, the gigantic figure of a man, carved in red stone, and holding in his hand seven wingless arrows. The ancient Arabs often drew lots to decide any important question, and for this purpose they used wingless arrows. Hubal was the oracle who presided over the drawing of lots.

The care of the Kaabah, with the duty of feeding the many pilgrims who came to worship at the holy shrine, was entrusted to the members of the tribe which had most power and influence; these also claimed the right of raising the banner and declaring war.

During the fifth and sixth centuries the ruling tribe at Meccah was the Kuraysh. This name is derived from a word which means "to trade," many of the leading members of the tribe having been great traders. The chief of the tribe of Kuraysh was the most important and influential man in Meccah. One of the most renowned of these chiefs was Hashim, who was born in A.D. 464; he was very rich, having gained great wealth by trading, and he did much to increase the prosperity of his native town. He instituted a regular caravan service between Meccah and the most important markets of the East; every winter a caravan set out for Yemen, and every summer for Syria. During the pilgrimage season, Hashim entertained the pilgrims with princely liberality, providing them with bread and meat, butter, barley, and dates. The ancient well Zem-Zem having long ago become choked up and the site forgotten, Hashim had large tanks made in which all the available water could be stored, thus giving Meccah a sufficient water-supply.

During the time that Hashim was chief of Meccah, there was a year of great scarcity, and the city was threatened with a serious famine. Hashim spent a great part of his wealth in relieving the wants of his fellow-countrymen; he travelled to Syria, and bought all the corn that could be collected; this was loaded on the backs of numerous camels and conveyed to Meccah to be distributed among the people. After this the camels were slaughtered and roasted, and plenty reigned in place of want and starvation.

Late in life Hashim married a noble lady of the town of Yathrib, and had a son who was named Shayba. While Shayba was yet but a child, Hashim died in Syria, where he had gone on a trading expedition. His younger brother, Muttalib, acted as chief of Meccah until Shayba was old enough to succeed to his father's dignities. In course of time Muttalib went to fetch Hashim's son from Yathrib, where he was living with his mother. When Muttalib returned to Meccah in company with the young lad, the people thought he had bought a slave, and called the boy Abd al-Muttalib, which means the slave, or the servant, of Muttalib. The name clung to him, and he is known in history by no other name than that of Abd al-Muttalib.

When he was old enough Hashim's son was installed in his father's place; but one of his uncles, whose name was Naufal, disputed his possession of the property and tried to rob the orphan of his rights. Abd al-Muttalib sent word to his mother's relations in Yathrib, letting them know how he had been treated. Thereupon eighty men of his mother's clan rode in haste to Meccah, and appeared before the Kaabah fully armed. Their chief, drawing his sword, threatened Naufal with instant death if he did not swear to respect the rights of his nephew Abd al-Muttalib. Naufal, overawed by this sudden boldness, swore a solemn oath in the presence of the assembled chiefs of the Kuraysh, agreeing to recognize the claims of Hashim's son.

For many years, however, Abd al-Muttalib had a hard struggle to retain his position, and he had many rivals who were jealous of his power. At last an event occurred which seemed to be the turning point in his fortunes. The site of Zem-Zem, the ancient well of Meccah, had, as I have already told you, been long forgotten. Abd al-Muttalib, having got some clue to its position, set himself diligently to find it. Long and patiently he continued excavating, with the help of his son, Harith. At last their efforts were rewarded, and they came on a quantity of treasure which had been buried in the well more than three hundred years before, during a tribal war. Two golden gazelles, some swords and suits of armour were discovered; the well was cleaned out, and found to contain an ample supply of water. Some of the other members of the tribe of Kuraysh disputed the right of Abd al-Muttalib both to the well and the treasure. Lots were cast with the arrows of Hubal to decide whether the newly found treasure should belong to Abd al-Muttalib, to the tribe of Kuraysh, or to the gods of the Kaabah. The drawing of the lots apportioned the golden gazelles to the Kaabah and the rest of the treasure to Abd al-Muttalib, while the arrows of the Kuraysh were blank. The gazelles were hammered out into plates of gold and nailed to the door of the Kaabah, and Abd al-Muttalib hung up the swords on the outside of the building to guard the treasures within.

From this time the fortunes of the chief steadily improved, his wealth increased, and he became famous, as his father Hashim had been before him, for the liberality with which he entertained the pilgrims. As guardian of the well Zem-Zem, it was also his duty to supply them with water. Thus Abd al-Muttalib acquired power and influence. But amid all his prosperity there was one thing which seriously troubled his peace of mind. In the East, people think a great deal of having many sons to succeed them and uphold the honour of the family. During the time of his long struggle with fortune, Abd al-Muttalib had but one son to help him, and in those days he had made a rash vow, for he had sworn before the gods of the Kaabah that if he ever possessed ten sons he would show his gratitude by offering up one of them in sacrifice. Years passed, several sons and daughters were born to Abd al-Muttalib, and at last the fatal number was reached. He was the father of ten sons, and the youngest, whose name was Abdallah, was his best beloved. For a long time Abd al-Muttalib delayed the fulfilment of his vow, which he now bitterly repented, but an oath sworn before the gods could not be lightly regarded. The day arrived when the sorrowing father took his ten sons with him to the Kaabah; each of their names was inscribed on a wingless arrow, that the lots might decide which of the ten was to be offered up in sacrifice.

Great were the lamentations in the family of Abd al-Muttalib when the lots were drawn, and it was found that Abdallah, the youngest and best-beloved, was doomed to death. His sisters clung to him, weeping bitterly, begging that his life might be spared. The unhappy father, stricken with grief, vowed that he would sacrifice ten camels in the place of his son if the divining arrows should decide in Abdallah's favour. So the lots were cast between ten camels and the life of Abdallah, but again the fatal arrow fell to him. Abd al-Muttalib now doubled the number of camels—twenty camels against the life of his son! But fate seemed determined not to spare him; again and again the lots decreed that Abdallah should die, and each time Abd al-Muttalib vowed ten camels more, until the number reached a hundred! The distracted father now waited in an agony of suspense while once again the lots were cast—a hundred camels against the life of Abdallah!

Fate at length relented, reversing her decree, and this time the arrow of death fell to the lot of the camels. These were slaughtered, and all the meat given away to the poor, for the family of Abd al-Muttalib refused to touch Abdallah's ransom. Released from his cruel doom, the boy was restored to his family; in course of time he became the father of Mohammed the Prophet.

When he was twenty-four years of age, Abdallah was married to Aminah, a maiden belonging to a distant branch of his own tribe, the Kuraysh. The year following their marriage was an important one in the history of Meccah. A large army advanced upon the city from the south, led by Abraha, viceroy of the king of Abyssinia, who at that time ruled in Yemen. Abraha rode at the head of his troops on a huge elephant, and the sight so impressed the Arabs that the year A.D. 570, in which these events occurred, has ever since been known as the Year of the Elephant. The invading army was stricken by a deadly disease and retired.

But another event, of vastly greater importance, happened in the Year of the Elephant; for in that year was born Mohammed, the son of Abdallah, destined to be the Prophet of Arabia.

The Youth of Mohammed

Great had been the rejoicings at the marriage of Abdallah and Aminah, but the happiness of the bridal pair was not to last long. A year had scarcely passed before Abdallah died, while on a visit to Yathrib, leaving to his sorrowing wife the care of her infant son.

Abd al-Muttalib had from the first taken a great interest in his little grandson. When told the news of his birth he had gone to the house of Aminah, and, taking the child in his arms, had carried him to the Kaabah, there to give thanks to God. The boy was named Mohammed, which means "The Praised," or "Illustrious."

It was the custom in Meccah to give young children into the care of Bedouin women, thus sending them away from the hot and dusty city into the pure air of the desert. The little Mohammed was nursed by a woman named Halimah, of the tribe of Banu Saad, and the first five years of his life were spent in the tents of this wandering tribe. All through his life, Mohammed remembered his Bedouin nurse and his foster-sister Al-Shaima, with tender affection. At the age of five he was brought back to Meccah by Halimah, who told his mother wonderful stories of the boy's early intelligence.

Aminah was very proud of her son, and anxious to show him to all his relations. When he was about six years old she took him to Yathrib, the place where Abdallah had died, and where his mother's relations lived. It was a long journey for so young a child, the distance being about the same as that between London and Edinburgh, but Arabs, with their wandering instincts, think very little of distance. Mounted on two camels, Aminah, her son, and a slave girl called Umm Ayman, accomplished the journey in safety. They spent a month in Yathrib, and Mohammed always looked back with pleasure to this time with his cousins. He amused himself with all sorts of childish games—years afterwards he remembered how he used to scare the pigeons from the roof of the house, screaming with delight as they circled away on flapping wings. He also learnt to swim in a pond.

A sad event was to follow this happy time. Aminah never returned to her home, for on the way back to Meccah she fell sick and died, and was buried at a place hall way between the two cities. Sorrowfully the orphan boy and Umm Ayman, the slave girl, continued their journey, and, having reached Meccah, they went to the house of Abd al-Muttalib to tell him the sad news. From this time Mohammed lived with his grandfather, of whom he grew very fond. Many a time would the boy run away from his nurse and take refuge with the old man, who never reproved him for these interruptions, for he had a tender affection for the orphan boy of his favourite son. No wonder that when, two years later, the Patriarch was carried to his grave, the little Mohammed wept as he followed the procession through the streets of Meccah. When on his death-bed, Abd al-Muttalib had entrusted the care of his grandson to Abu Talib, one of his elder sons, who soon became as devoted to the boy as his grandfather had been. Indeed, all through his life, Mohammed possessed the power of gaining the affections of those around him.

From an early age, the son of Abdallah had to work for his living, all the fortune he inherited from his father being a flock of goats, five camels, and Umm Ayman the slave girl; while his uncle, who was not rich, had little to spare from the needs of his large family. In his young days, Mohammed was often employed as a shepherd, and as he was of a thoughtful disposition the solitary life probably suited him. When he was twelve years old he had his first experience of a different world from that in which he had been brought up. Abu Talib, who was an enterprising merchant, was about to start on an expedition to Bostra, in Syria, when his nephew begged that he might be allowed to accompany him. Abu Talib, being very fond of the boy, consented, and Mohammed, in high glee, started on his first journey with a caravan.

The expectation of seeing new and strange sights must have been as exciting to Mohammed's imagination as it is to any boy's of the present day. But how different were the ways of travelling! To most of us a journey means a few hours in a comfortable railway carriage, or a pleasant time on board a luxurious liner. To a Meccan boy it meant many long and weary marches. Day after day, sitting on the back of a camel, he would travel at a slow pace through the same monotonous scenery. Sometimes the caravan would pass by a mud-built village, where barking watch-dogs would give warning of its approach; sometimes the route lay along the outskirts of the great desert, and here there would be few sights to break the monotony—perhaps a frightened gazelle scurrying across the track of the caravan, or an eagle soaring aloft in the burning blue.

Mohammed, who had a vivid imagination, found plenty to occupy his thoughts during the long journey to Bostra. Indeed, some of the impressions he received at this time remained with him all through his life. Many strange tales would be told round the camp fire when the caravan halted in some wild and lonely spot said to be haunted by spirits called *genii* or *jinns*. Sometimes the road passed the site of some ancient city of former splendour whose ruins were long since buried beneath the drifting sand. But of all he saw and heard, nothing so impressed the youthful mind of Mohammed as the stories about the Valley of Al-Hijr. Long ago this land had been inhabited by the tribe of Thamud, a people of a giant and powerful race. The Thamudites had grown rich and prosperous, until, being lifted up with pride, they had fallen into sin. Persisting in their wickedness, they refused to listen to the prophet who was sent to warn them, and, by an act of direct disobedience, called down on themselves the judgment of God. Loud claps of thunder were heard, announcing that the vengeance of Heaven was near, and when morning dawned every man lay dead, with his face turned downward. Thus was the tribe of Thamud swept from off the face of the earth, and upon the land it had occupied was pronounced an everlasting curse. This story impressed Mohammed with deep awe, and, as the caravan passed along the lonely valley, he was shown the rock dwellings which the giants of the tribe of Thamud had hewn out of the mountain side. When, after years, Mohammed travelled to Syria by the same route he forbade his followers to encamp anywhere near the place where judgment had overtaken the

Mohammed And His Nurse Halimah.

Thamudites, or to use the water from the wells of the neighbourhood. Indeed, few could enter the accursed vale of Al-Hijr without a feeling of dread, and travellers would hurry along the wind-swept passes the quicker to escape from that land of evil fame.

At length, Mohammed reached his journey's end and arrived at Bostra, where the caravan was encamped near a monastery of Christian monks. Some weeks passed while the merchandise from Meccah and the south was exchanged for the goods of Syria, Persia or Egypt, for Bostra was the meeting-place of merchants from many distant lands. When the camels had again been loaded, and provisions for the journey prepared, the caravan started on its way south, and in due time reached Meccah once more.

Thirteen years later, when Mohammed had reached the age of twenty-five, he was again on his way to Bostra. This time he was himself the leader of the caravan and entrusted with the buying and selling of the merchandise. The owner of this caravan was a rich widow named Khadijah, who lived in Meccah. When inquiring for an agent to manage her affairs and conduct her caravans, she heard such good accounts of the trustworthiness and fair dealing of young Mohammed that she engaged him as her steward.

Mohammed returned from Syria with such good value for the goods he had exchanged that Khadijah gave him double the wages she had promised him. She had every reason to be satisfied with her steward, whose honest and upright character was so well known that his fellow-citizens had surnamed him Al-Amin, or the Faithful.

Indeed, this young man with his earnest expression and open, straightforward manner had made a great impression on Khadijah. We are told that Mohammed was attractive in appearance. He had the fine, rather thin, features of the true Arab, his eyes were very dark and piercing, and he had a way of gazing straight into the face of the person he was addressing. His hair and beard were jet black. Though usually inclined to be silent, Mohammed could be witty and amusing when conversing with his friends, and he knew how to laugh. His movements showed decision, and his footstep was said to be like that of a man rapidly descending a hill.

Khadijah seems to have early understood Mohammed's true and generous nature, and as time passed the widow's regard for her steward grew into affection. Once, when the return of the caravan was expected, Khadijah and her maidens were sitting on the house-top in the cool of the evening to watch for the first glimpse of the long string of camels winding down the rocky valley. As the caravan came in sight, Khadijah's eye fell on a single rider, and she recognized Mohammed, who was hastening in advance of the rest to report the safe return and success of the expedition. After their interview Khadijah's thoughts dwelt constantly on the young man; she could not forget him, and at length resolved to make her affection known to him.

Khadijah was a wealthy lady of the tribe of Kuraysh; several of the leading chiefs of Meccah had sought to marry her, but she had rejected their offers. Her choice now fell on the young son of Abdallah; though she was considerably older than he was, they were married and lived happily together for many years. Six children were born to them, two sons, who both died at an early age, and four daughters, whose names were Zainab, Rukayyah, Umm Kulthum, and Fatimah. Fatimah, her father's favourite, and the only one who outlived him, is the one we shall hear most about.

The early years of Mohammed's married life were quiet and uneventful. The rebuilding of the Kaabah, which took place about ten years after his marriage, was the most important event of this time. A violent storm had flooded the valley of Meccah, causing great damage to the ancient temple. The walls were unsafe, and, after some discussion, it was decided to pull them down and rebuild them. For this purpose great blocks of granite were carried down from the neighbouring hills, but timber, which was required for the roof and the interior, was very scarce in that barren land. It was therefore a fortunate event for the builders of the Kaabah when a Greek ship was wrecked on the coast of the Red Sea within fairly easy distance of Meccah. All the timber from the wreck was bought by the Kuraysh, and the ship's captain, who had some knowledge of architecture, was engaged to help in the rebuilding of the Kaabah. When the walls of the temple had reached the height of four or five feet, an important matter had to be decided. The sacred and mysterious Black Stone was now to be fixed in its place, but so many of the families of the Kuraysh claimed the honour of doing this, that a violent discussion arose and the building was stopped for several days. Who was to settle this difficult question? The dispute still continued, when one of the citizens suggested that the first man who entered the court of the Kaabah by the eastern gate should be asked to decide which of the many claimants deserved the honour of replacing the Black Stone. This proposal was agreed to, and all eyes were turned toward the gate in question. Presently a man was seen approaching. "Here is Al-Amin!" cried the citizens, as Mohammed passed through the gate, "let him judge between us!"

Mohammed, on being asked to settle the dispute, took off his cloak, spread it on the ground, and placed the Black Stone upon it. He then directed that four men (one from each of the chief clans of the Kuraysh) should together lift the cloak with its precious burden. When the Black Stone had been raised to the required height from the ground, Mohammed himself set it in its place in the southeast corner of the temple.

After this incident, the building of the Kaabah was continued without interruption. When all was complete, the images of the gods were restored to their places; Hubal, the most honoured, being placed in a central position in the interior of the Kaabah. Little did the Kuraysh foresee the day when the gods of their fathers would be held up to scorn and denounced as vain idols! The quiet and retiring citizen, Al-Amin, had as yet shown no sign of the high destiny that awaited him.

Mohammed as a Prophet

For many years after his marriage, Mohammed led a quiet and peaceful life with his devoted wife, Khadijah. He was now a rich man, and a respected citizen of his native town. Always of a thoughtful nature, he grew more inclined to solitude and retirement, and, as time went on, he began to reflect on the idolatry of his countrymen, searching in his mind for a purer religion. He was not the only one who realized the sinfulness of idolatry; there were other serious-minded men who practised the ancient religion of Abraham, which means that they worshipped one God, whom they called the Most High God (Allah ta' alah). During the month of Ramadan, which seems, even in those early days, to have been set apart as a time for fasting and religious observance, these holy men would retire to solitary places for prayer and meditation.

At the head of a sandy valley not far from Mecca stands a high cone-shaped mountain. In old days it was called Mount Hira, but its name was afterwards changed to Jebel Nur, or the Mountain of Light, for it was there that Mohammed first saw the light that was to lead his people into the way of truth. The view from this mountain is wild and desolate—peaks of grey and black rock, of curious and fantastic shapes, rise, one above the other, in solemn grandeur, while no speck of green relieves the barrenness of the outlook. The mountains of Arabia, like those of Northern Africa, have not the soft outlines of many of our hills at home, but are deeply furrowed and wrinkled, as though great age had left its mark upon them.

Some way up the steep side of Mount Hira is a cave to which Mohammed often retired for solitary meditation, and sometimes Khadijah, his wife, would accompany him to this quiet retreat. For Mohammed was passing through a time of doubt and perplexity, he longed for the Truth, which he felt was not to be found in the worship of idols, but, as yet, the way was not clear to his mind. We must remember that Mohammed was never in a position to learn all that our religion has taught us; he may, from time to time, have met with a few Christians, but the Christianity that found its way into Arabia in those days had lost much of its purity. Nevertheless, when he had firmly grasped the idea that "God is One, the Eternal," that "there is none like unto Him," Mohammed had got far on the way leading to Truth. The Unity of God is the one great outstanding doctrine of the Mohammedan faith. That he should have been chosen to preach this doctrine to mankind dawned by slow degrees on Mohammed's mind. This is how it came about.

It was the month of Ramadan, and Mohammed had gone to the cave on Mount Hira, to devote this time to prayer and fasting. Unusually excited by his thoughts, he fell into a trance and saw a vision. On the far horizon he beheld the form of the Archangel Gabriel—nearer and nearer he approached until he stood within two bows' lengths of Mohammed. Holding out a scroll, the Angel commanded him to "Read!" "But I cannot read," said Mohammed, trembling before the heavenly vision. Three times the Angel cried "Read!" and then he recited the words that were written on the scroll, proclaiming the greatness of God, the Creator of mankind.

Mohammed was much troubled by this vision or dream, doubting whether he had indeed received a divine revelation, or whether he might have been deceived and in the power of evil spirits. For days together he would wander alone among the rocks of Mount Hira, trying to solve the doubts that oppressed him; so distracted was his mind at this time that he was sometimes tempted to throw himself from one of the steep crags into the abyss below, and so end the struggle. But an invisible hand seemed to hold him back, and for nearly three years he endured the agony of uncertainty.

But at length, Mohammed had another vision; Gabriel appeared to him a second time, and he heard a voice crying, "Arise and preach, and magnify thy Lord!" From this time all doubts and difficulties left him, and Mohammed felt assured that he was chosen to be the prophet of his people. What he actually saw, or thought he saw, matters little; the important thing is this: that to his own mind the visions were true ones,

MOHAMMED'S VISION

that he firmly believed he had a divine message to deliver to mankind, and this conviction deeply influenced his actions until his dying day.

So with all the strength and determination that was in him, Mohammed set himself to preach the worship of the True God. He did not pretend that the religion he taught was something new, but called it the faith of Abraham, and the particular name he gave it was Islam, which signifies "striving after righteousness." We usually call Mohammed's followers Mohammedans, after his own name, and they are also called Moslems. In the end Mohammed succeeded in banishing idolatry from Arabia, but many trials and difficulties were to be overcome before that time arrived.

When he began his public preaching, Mohammed was about forty-four years old. Very little progress was made during the earlier years of his mission. The first to believe in him as a prophet was his beloved wife Khadijah, who had given her husband all the help and sympathy in her power during the years of doubt and trial. Another early believer was Zaid, who had been Mohammed's slave, and whom he had freed and adopted as a son. When Zaid was a young child he had fallen into the hands of some wandering Arabs, who had carried him off and sold him as a slave, and it so happened that he was given to Khadijah soon after her marriage with Mohammed. Zaid's father, overcome with grief for the loss of his son, searched for him far and wide, but it was many years before he heard of him from some men of his tribe who had been to Meccah for the pilgrimage. The delighted father set out at once and journeyed to Meccah with the intention of ransoming his son from slavery, but Zaid refused to leave his master, who, he said, had been as father and mother to him. Mohammed, touched by this devotion, took Zaid to the Kaabah, the ancient temple of Meccah, and publicly adopted him as a son. Zaid's father, satisfied with this arrangement, went home, leaving his son in Mohammed's care.

There was another inmate of the Prophet's house who was one of the early converts to Islam; this was Ali, the son of Abu Talib, Mohammed's kind protector. Abu Talib was a poor man, and had many children to provide for, so Mohammed, to help his uncle, adopted one of his sons. We shall hear a good deal about Ali; he was of a brave and noble nature, and remained loyal to his faith during many years of struggle and trial. There were a few other conversions during these early days, the most important being that of Abu Bakr.

Abu Bakr was a rich merchant about two years younger than Mohammed, of whom he was a devoted friend. He was a small, thin man, with a kindly and thoughtful expression, and was fairer than most Arabs. Most generous with his money, he gave away a great deal to the poor, and was always ready to help the weak and oppressed. On account of his faithful and honest nature, Abu Bakr was surnamed "Al Siddick," or "The True"; his friendship for Mohammed remained unchanged to the end of the Prophet's life. It was a great advantage to the new faith that such a good and respected man as Abu Bakr should join the small band of believers, and several others soon followed his example.

But the greater number of the people of Meccah, and especially those of Mohammed's own tribe, the Kuraysh, would give no heed to his teaching; he threatened them with the vengeance of Heaven if they refused to give up their idols and lead better lives, but the men of the Kuraysh only scoffed at him and began to persecute the Believers. They were specially hard on the converted slaves and the strangers who were not under the protection of a chief.

These were cruelly ill-treated, being sometimes seized, bound hand and foot, and left, without a drop of water, in the scorching sun, until they would acknowledge the idols of Meccah. Many could not stand this severe trial of their faith, and were forced to give in, though they afterwards returned, repentant, to the Prophet.

Among these sufferers was a tall, powerful Abyssinian slave named Bilal; although nearly dying of thirst, he remained true to his faith, resolutely refusing to say a word against the Prophet. One day, when Bilal had been exposed for many hours in the burning sun, Abu Bakr happened to pass by; he bought the faithful slave, had him released from his fetters and gave him his freedom. Bilal afterwards became famous as the first muezzin; the muezzin is the crier who announces the hours of prayer from a mosque, and Bilal, having a very powerful voice, was chosen for this office.

Abu Bakr did all he could to relieve the sufferings of the oppressed Believers, and soon spent the greater part of his wealth in buying persecuted slaves in order to set them free. As yet, the Kuraysh did not dare to interfere with important persons and chiefs, or those who were under their protection. Thus Mohammed himself, being a member of the ruling tribe, and under the protection of his uncle, Abu Talib, an elder of the tribe, was, for a time, left unmolested. But the less favoured Believers suffered so much from the ill-treatment of the Kuraysh that Mohammed advised them to take refuge in a foreign country. About twenty Moslems emigrated to Abyssinia; among them was Mohammed's daughter, Rukayyah, and her husband, Othman, who was a merchant. The exiles were kindly received by the Christian king of Abyssinia, who realized that the new faith had much in common with Christianity. For Mohammed taught his followers kindness and compassion to their fellow-creatures and also to animals. He enjoined the merchants to be fair and honest in their dealings, and he insisted on the duties of feeding the hungry, visiting the sick, and giving alms to the poor.

The struggle between Mohammed and the Kuraysh became very bitter; the Prophet openly denounced the idols of Meccah, and exhorted the people to repentance, telling them that God would punish them if they did not forsake their sins. The elders of the Kuraysh, furious that the gods of their fathers should be thus insulted, now went to Abu Talib and complained that his nephew was disturbing the peace of Meccah. They demanded that the Chief should order Mohammed to give up preaching in public, and refuse any longer to give him his protection if he would not agree to their terms. Abu Talib, though not a believer, was very fond of his nephew, whom he had always regarded as a son, and was anxious that no harm should happen to him. So he sent for Mohammed and told him of the complaints of the Kuraysh; he might hold what opinions he pleased, said the Chief, who was now a very old man, but he must not declare them openly. Mohammed answered, "If they brought the sun on my right hand and the moon on my left, bidding me cease from my undertaking, I would give no heed, unless the Lord should command me." He was so grieved at the trouble he had caused his kind protector that he burst into tears and turned to depart. But Abu Talib called him back, assuring him that he would never desert him, and bade him do whatever he considered his duty. It was very noble of Abu Talib thus to stand by his nephew against the chief men of his tribe, for he was not himself a convert, and it is doubtful if he ever became one.

Two more sons had been born to Abd al-Muttalib in his old age; their names were Hamzah and Abbas. Hamzah, who was about the same age as the Prophet, was famous as a hunter, of great courage and strength; he was also remarkable for his good looks, and was a favourite with all who knew him. One day, as he was returning from a hunting expedition, with his bow slung across his shoulder, he heard that Mohammed had been openly insulted by Abu Jahl, one of his bitterest enemies. The Prophet had not answered a word, while Abu Jahl had reviled and jeered at him. Hamzah, enraged at this insult to his nephew, went straight to the Kaabah, where he found Abu Jahl sitting with the chiefs of Meccah. Burning with just anger, Hamzah struck Abu Jahl violently with his bow, and, on the impulse of the moment, declared himself a Moslem. He remained true to the Faith, and in after years fought so valiantly in the defence of Islam that he was surnamed the Lion of God.

Nearly all religions have their sacred books. The sacred book of the Mohammedans is called the Koran; it is the work of the Prophet Mohammed, and was written, or dictated, by him at different times during his prophetic career. The word Koran means, in Arabic, the Reading, as our word Bible means the Book. Mohammed believed that the words of the Koran were divinely revealed to him, and, indeed, every great work which comes from the deepest convictions of a man's soul may be said to be so inspired.

In his early days as a shepherd, Mohammed had lived much with nature; he had seen the pale dawn touch the grim summits of Mount Hira and Mount Arafat, had heard the thunder roll through the sounding passes of the hills, had felt the icy breath of the desert wind when the rocks were aflame with the glow of sunset. In all the wonders of nature, he felt the presence of a Mighty Creator. "The sun in his early splendour, the moon when she followeth him, the day when it showeth forth his glory"—these things filled the soul of Mohammed with awe and admiration. "Surely these are signs of the greatness of God, if ye would but read them!" he would say to the unbelievers.

The judgment day was, for Mohammed, not a dim prophecy, but a great reality, whose image was never absent from his mind: in one of the early chapters of the Koran we read:

"When the Heaven is rent asunder
And when the stars are scattered,
And when the seas are let loose,
And when the tombs are turned upside down,
The soul shall know what it hath done and left undone."

Mohammed attached great importance to prayer, calling it the gate of heaven. But he warned his followers that the prayers of those who only pray with their lips and not with their whole hearts would not be accepted by God. "Woe to those who pray and who are careless in their prayers." Outward observances count for nothing in themselves. "There is no piety," said the Prophet, "in turning your faces towards the East or West, but he is pious who believeth in God."

The opening chapter of the Koran is regarded with special reverence by Moslems, who use it as one of their daily prayers. It reads as follows:

"Praise be to God, the Lord of the Worlds!
The Compassionate, the Merciful!
King of the day of Judgment!
Thee we worship, and Thee we ask for help.
Guide us in the straight way,
The way of those to whom Thou art gracious;
Not of those upon whom is Thy wrath nor of the erring."

The Year of Mourning

In the sixth year of Mohammed's mission there was a second emigration to Abyssinia, where the Moslems soon numbered over a hundred. But in spite of persecutions, the little band of Believers at Meccah was steadily increasing; one or two men of influence were added to its numbers, and at one time Mohammed even had hopes of the conversion of a Chief of the Kuraysh. One day when the Prophet was in earnest conversation with this Chief, a poor blind man came up and interrupted him. "O Apostle of God," cried Abdallah, the blind man, "teach me some part of what God hath taught thee!" But the Prophet, annoyed at the interruption, frowned and turned away. This incident is alluded to in the Koran, and we realize Mohammed's generous nature in his readiness to confess a fault and own himself in the wrong. "The Prophet frowned and turned aside, because the blind man came to him. ... The man who is wealthy, thou receivest respectfully ... but him who cometh unto thee earnestly seeking his salvation, and who feareth God, dost thou neglect. By no means shouldest thou act thus."

On account of the insulting behaviour of their enemies the Moslems had, for some time past, given up praying in public; they used to meet secretly in the house of a convert named Al-Arkam. This house, situated on the hill of Safa, away from the centre of the town, came to be known as the "House of Islam."

It was not long after Hamzah had declared himself a Moslem that another important conversion was made. Mohammed's enemy, Abu Jahl, had a nephew called Omar, who was, at the time of which we are speaking, twenty-six years of age. He was of gigantic height, and so bold and strong that his fellow-citizens were more afraid of his walking staff than of other men's swords, while his hasty temper made him a terror to his enemies Omar bitterly opposed the Moslems, and some say that he had agreed with Abu Jahl to waylay the Prophet and stab him. One day, a rumour reached Omar that his sister Ramlah had been converted to the new religion. Full of wrath, he went straight to his sister's house to discover the truth. Entering hurriedly, he found Ramlah and her husband, Said, listening to a reading of the Koran. Omar, in a furious passion, drew his sword, and turning on his brother-in-law, felled him to the ground, while Ramlah, throwing herself between the combatants, was wounded by the point of her brother's sword.

When Omar saw the blood flowing from his sister's face he was struck with shame, his fury was subdued, and he asked to see the scroll from which the reading was taken. But Ramlah would not allow him to touch it until he had washed and purified himself, as the Moslems are in the habit of doing before prayers. When this had been done, Omar took the scroll and began to read the twentieth chapter of the Koran: "We have not sent the Koran unto thee that thou shouldest be unhappy; but for a warning unto him who feareth God. ... The Merciful sitteth on His throne: unto Him belongeth whatsoever is in heaven and earth, and whatsoever is between them, and whatsoever is under the earth. If thou pronounce thy prayers with a loud voice, know that it is not necessary, for God knoweth that which is secret, and what is hidden." Omar realized that these were not the words of a madman; as he read further the truth sank deep into his soul, and he asked to be taken to the Prophet that he might declare himself a Believer.

The Faithful were gathered together in the house of Al-Arkam when a knock was heard on the door. Hamzah, before opening it, peeped through a crevice, and when he announced that Omar stood without, several of the Moslems drew their swords, ready to defend the Prophet, and bar the way to the intruder. But Mohammed bade him enter, and great was his joy when Omar made his profession of faith. From that day he devoted himself to the Prophet's cause, and, like St. Paul, became a brave defender of the faith he had persecuted. The day after his conversion, Omar went boldly to the Kaabah to pray, the other Moslems following his example, and such was the fear inspired by Omar's strong arm and fiery temper that none dared interfere.

Like Abu Bakr, Omar became one of the Prophet's chief advisers; in

BILAL CALLING THE MOSLEMS TO PRAYER.

after years they both succeeded him as head of Islam, or Khalif, a word which means Successor. We realize how great was Mohammed's influence over his fellowmen when we learn that the mild and retiring Abu Bakr became a bold leader in time of war, and the hasty and violent Omar a wise and moderate ruler.

The Kuraysh, alarmed at the recent conversions, determined to take strong measures to crush this new faith which threatened to overthrow the ancient religion of their forefathers. At a council of, the elders it was decided that Mohammed and all those who took his part against the rest of the tribe of Kuraysh should be outlawed. All rights of citizenship were to be denied them, no one might sell them food, marry into their families, or have any kind of dealings with them. This decree, or Ban, as it was called, was written on a piece of parchment, which was sealed with three seals and hung up inside the Kaabah. All Mohammed's near relations, even those who were not believers, rallied round him, with the exception of one of his uncles—Abu Lahab. In fact, the greater number of the descendants of Hashim, Mohammed's great grandfather, stood by their kinsman. But the Hashimites, as they were called, could not hope to hold their own against the rest of the tribe of Kuraysh; some were openly attacked, the Prophet himself was one day seized in the Kaabah, and would have been strangled had he not been bravely rescued by Abu Bakr, who was wounded in the struggle.

The mountains on the eastern side of Mecca rise very steeply, like cliffs, quite close to the town, and between their spurs are long narrow ravines called Shebs. The word Sheb means, in Arabic, a rock. The outskirts of the city extended right into these ravines, in one of which was a castle, or stronghold, belonging to Abu Talib. Enclosed by steep rocks on every side, there was, from this Sheb, but one opening communicating with the town, and this was a gateway, so narrow that a camel could only just pass through it.

In the Sheb of Abu Talib, the Hashimites took refuge from their persecutors. It was no longer safe for them to live in the city, for every time they left their houses, they ran the risk of being attacked by their oppressors. Khadijah, the Prophet's devoted wife, and all the members of his household, shared his exile; even his uncles, with the exception of Abu Lahab, left their homes and followed Mohammed into the Sheb. Many of the descendants of Hashim were not believers, but the feeling of kinship, which is very strong among the Arabs, induced them to take the side of the Prophet against the leaders of the Kuraysh. You will understand that the name Kuraysh applies to the whole tribe; while the Hashimites were a clan of that tribe: we cannot but admire the loyalty of Mohammed's relations in thus sharing his hardships.

For nearly three years, the Hashimites remained in the Sheb of Abu Talib. They suffered cruel privation and want, for corn soon became very scarce, and the Hashimites were not rich enough to send out caravans of their own, while the merchants who came to Meccah were prevented, by the Kuraysh, from having any dealings with the outlaws. There were times when the unfortunate Hashimites were on the verge of starvation, the wailing of the hungry babies could be heard in the city, and many, even of the Kuraysh, were moved to compassion, and thought the terms of the Ban too hard. But the Elders were determined to suppress the new faith, and had no thought of giving in. A nephew of Khadijah had sometimes found means of sending supplies to his aunt, and on one occasion a camel laden with corn was brought secretly into the Sheb by night; but those who gave help to the sufferers ran the risk of offending the Chiefs of Meccah, by breaking the rules of the Ban.

There was one time in the year when the outlaws could, with safety, leave their retreat. This was the month in which the yearly pilgrimage to the Kaabah took place; it was regarded by the Arabs as a sacred month, during which all feuds were suspended. Caravans crossing the desert had no fear of plunderers, and warring tribes were at peace with one another, for the truce of the holy month was observed throughout Arabia. Thus it came about that the season of pilgrimage was also the time when the great fairs were held, both at Meccah and other places in the neighbourhood.

When, therefore, the time of pilgrimage came round the Hashimites were able, once more, to mix with their fellow-citizens. Mohammed took every advantage of these peaceful intervals in renewing his efforts to gain converts. He went to several of the great fairs, and amid the noisy confusion of the buyers and sellers preached against the sin of idolatry whenever he could find listeners. But he was received for the most part with hoots and jeers. "Why do not your own countrymen believe in you if you are a true prophet?" cried the strangers. One is struck with wonder at Mohammed's persistence and fortitude; no discouragement seemed to weaken his fixed resolve to establish the faith he felt himself commissioned to preach. The Kuraysh would, at any moment, have allowed Mohammed to return to his home and live the life of a peaceful citizen, if he would have agreed to give up preaching his doctrines. This, however, he resolutely refused to do. When the month of pilgrimage was over, the rules of the Ban were again enforced in all their strictness, and the Hashimites returned to the Sheb of Abu Talib. During the third year of their imprisonment an incident occurred which changed the course of events.

Rumours reached Mohammed that the parchment on which the Ban was written had been destroyed by insects, and he took this as a sign that God had favoured his cause. So Abu Talib, with a few companions, went to the Kaabah, and standing before the Chiefs and Elders, addressed them thus: "I am told that the parchment has been devoured by insects; if this be true, you should cancel the rules of the Ban, and let the Hashimites go free. But if you can prove that I have spoken falsely, I will deliver my nephew into your hands."

These terms were agreed to, and the parchment was fetched from the Kaabah, while all waited in suspense for the issue. When the parchment was unrolled, it was found that most of it had been eaten away by white ants, and the rules of the Ban were unreadable. An Arab historian relates that the only word which was still visible was the name of God.

Abu Talib, satisfied that he had spoken the truth, bitterly reproached the Kuraysh for their cruel treatment of their countrymen, and without waiting to hear their decision, departed and returned to the Sheb. But as soon as he had gone five Chiefs of the Kuraysh stood up and declared the Ban to be at an end. They put on their armour and made their way to the Sheb of Abu Talib, to announce to the outlaws the joyful news that they might return to their homes in safety. Though many of the Kuraysh disapproved of these measures, they were forced to submit to the terms they had agreed to.

What a relief must it have been to the exiles to leave the narrow ravine in which they had been so long imprisoned, and to return in peace to their homes! The house in which Mohammed and Khadijah lived is still to be seen. But not long was the Prophet to be free from care, for he had soon to endure a bitter sorrow. Before many months had passed, his beloved wife, Khadijah, died. Mohammed was so overcome with grief that he at first refused all comfort. Well was Khadijah named "The Mother of the Believers," for had she not stood by the Prophet in his hour of trial and given him her help and counsel, had she not encouraged him and suffered with him when the future of Islam seemed wellnigh hopeless! It has been said that without Khadijah, Mohammed would never have become a Prophet. In the ancient cemetery lying on the western slope of the mountains north of Meccah Khadijah's grave is still to be seen. When, in after years, Mohammed had several wives, according to Arab custom, he was once asked by the young and beautiful Ayesha if she were not better than Khadijah. "No, by Heaven," answered Mohammed, "she believed in me when no one else did, she enriched me when I was poor, she was true to me when all the rest of the world was against me."

Yet another sorrow befell the Prophet about this time. It was scarcely five weeks after Khadijah's death that lost his uncle and protector, Abu Talib. Mohammed was now indeed desolate, for he had lost the two best friends he ever had—the wife who had been his trusted counsellor for twenty-five years, and the uncle who had acted as a father towards him since his boyhood. With good reason was the year in which these events took place called the Year of Mourning.

The Pledge of Al-Akabah

Ten years had passed since Mohammed had been ordered to "Arise and Preach!" To the best of his power he had striven to obey what he believed to be his Lord's commands; but he had met with insults, ridicule, and such opposition as would have deterred any man not possessing a firm belief in the righteousness of his cause. This period of waiting is the most wonderful part of Mohammed's whole career; he had nothing to support him but his own faith in his cause, yet even when his prospects were darkest he never for a moment doubted that God would help him to accomplish the task He had given him. The extraordinary grit and endurance of Mohammed's nature were put to the utmost test during this time of trial and disappointment. There could have been no thought of worldly ambition in his mind, for Mohammed was a rich man, a member of the ruling tribe, and might have risen to a high position in the administration of his native town. He chose, however, to pursue a course which brought on him the enmity of the most powerful of the Meccan chiefs.

After Abu Talib's death, the Prophet's opponents became bolder, and offered him such insults as they would not have dared during the Chief's lifetime. The people jeered at him and pelted him with dirt as he passed through the streets. When one of the Prophet's daughters wept to see her father so ill-used, he comforted her, saying, "Weep not, for truly the Lord will be thy father's helper." Life at Meccah became intolerable for Mohammed, and despairing of making any impression on his own countrymen, he began to think of planting the faith in some other place.

Eastward of Meccah, and distant about seventy miles, there is a city called Taif; might not the people of Taif be persuaded of the Truth, even though the Meccans refused to hear the Prophet who had been sent to them! It was scarcely a fortnight after Abu Talib's death that Mohammed set out to walk to Taif. He was accompanied by Zaid, whom I have mentioned as an adopted son of the Prophet, and one of the earliest converts to Islam. Mohammed left Meccah with a heavy heart. All his hopes and all his happiness seemed to be buried in his native city; those who had been closely bound to him by ties of affection and gratitude lay in their graves, while the hopes which had arisen in his heart of becoming the saviour of his people had been defeated. How long it seemed since he had wandered in the solitudes of Mount Hira, questioning his own soul, until convinced of his mission to preach! How he had laboured and striven to establish his cause, disregarding ease and wealth, and, when disheartened, supported by Khadijah's ready sympathy. The labours of those ten years seemed to have borne little fruit, when now, at the age of fifty, Mohammed was leaving his native town secretly, on foot, and all but a fugitive!

The first forty miles of the road from Meccah to Taif lie along barren and rocky valleys; great boulders are strewn along the path, and it is a long and weary climb to the heights of Mount Korah. Looking backward, the prospect is desolate in the extreme, but, where the road descends on the other side of the mountain chain, a very different picture meets the eye. Several streams flow from the summit of Mount Korah, fertilizing the lower ground, and here large sycamores, springing up between the granite rocks, give a pleasant shade, while figs, vines, apricots, peaches and pomegranates grow in abundance. What a contrast to the stony deserts round Meccah, and how must the weary spirits of the travellers have been refreshed by such a scene!

On arriving at Taif, Mohammed went in search of the chief men of the place, and explained to them the mission on which he had come to their city. But he soon discovered that his hopes of persuading the men of Taif to support his cause were utterly vain.

There was at Taif a famous idol, Al-Lat; it was a large stone figure in the shape of a woman, and was covered with precious stones. This idol was supposed to be mysteriously inspired with life, and was regarded with great awe by the people of Taif. When they discovered the purpose of Mohammed's visit, they turned on him with fury, refusing to hear him speak, and finally drove him from their city by pelting him with stones. Both Zaid and the Prophet received severe wounds, and were forced to retreat, the mob pursuing them for about three miles across the sandy plain. Weary and dispirited, the fugitives rested in an orchard near some gardens which happened to belong to some of the Kuraysh. For several of the rich men of that tribe owned houses and gardens near Taif, which they used as summer resorts. It so happened that two of these men had seen the Prophet's wretched plight, and, having compassion on him, they sent him a dish of grapes by a Christian slave, who was much struck by Mohammed's noble resignation under the humiliating treatment he had just received.

The travellers now retraced their steps towards Meccah, but Mohammed dared not enter the city until he had been assured of the protection of one of the chiefs, for his position was more that of a hunted outlaw than a free citizen. While, therefore, Zaid went forward to arrange matters, Mohammed waited in the valley of Nakhla, midway between Meccah and Taif. Though there were a few houses in this valley, it was a wild and desolate spot, such a place as was believed by the Arabs to be haunted by Jinns, or spirits of fire. The Jinns were regarded as beings midway between men and angels; they were made of pure fire, while man was made of clay, but, like man, they could sin, and stood in need of salvation. When Mohammed rose during the night to pray and recite portions of the Koran, he believed himself surrounded by a great company of these spirits, who listened eagerly to his words. And the heart of the prophet was comforted in the thought that, though men refused to hear him, his message was understood by the spirits of fire.

After a while, Mohammed received word that one of the five chiefs who had declared the Ban at an end promised to protect him, and he therefore returned to Meccah. This Chief, who was of Mohammed's tribe, went, in full armour, to the Kaabah, mounted on his camel, and, in the presence of the leaders of the Kuraysh, pledged himself to protect the Prophet, and to avenge any injury that might be done to him. But notwithstanding this promise of protection, Mohammed enjoyed little security in his native town. The cause of Islam seemed well-nigh hopeless, and the Moslems remaining in Meccah (for many were still

MOHAMMED PELTED AND JEERED AT IN THE STREETS

in Abyssinia) dared not practise their religion openly, as their enemies were too strong for them.

About this time, Mohammed married a second wife, named Sauda, who was the widow of an Abyssinian emigrant. He was also betrothed to Ayesha, the daughter of his friend Abu Bakr, but, as she was still very young, the marriage did not take place till three years later.

When the prospects of Islam were at their darkest an incident occurred which inspired Mohammed with fresh hopes. It was during the time of the great pilgrimage that he fell into conversation with some pilgrims from Yathrib, a town, as you may remember, lying to the north of MeccA, and about 270 miles distant. It was to this town that Mohammed went with his mother when a young child. Several Jewish tribes were settled at Yathrib, so the Arabs who came in contact with them were familiar with a faith which taught the worship of One God, and condemned idolatry. They were therefore more inclined to look with favour on Mohammed's doctrines than were his own countrymen.

The fame of the Prophet who had so disturbed the peace of Mecca had been carried to Yathrib by the caravans that halted there on their way to Syria, so when the pilgrims met Mohammed in the Valley of Mina (close to Mecca) they were eager to hear what he had to say. Deeply impressed by the doctrine of the new faith, several professed themselves believers; but they told the Prophet that they could not invite him to come to their city, as, owing to constant feuds between the tribes, they would be unable to protect him. For Yathrib was at that time, in a state of unrest, the two chief tribes, the Aus and the Khazraj, were constantly at war with each other. The Jews sometimes took the side of the one, sometimes of the other, while the many jealousies between the rival tribes prevented their ever uniting under a single leader. In these circumstances Yathrib was not a place where the Prophet was likely to find a safe refuge, but the pilgrims promised to consult with their fellow-citizens, and they arranged to meet the Prophet the following year, at the time of Pilgrimage, to tell him how matters stood.

A year is a long time to wait for an event on which great issues depend, but in the East men are less impatient than we are, and Mohammed, who had already waited so many years, could well wait another, with fresh hopes to encourage him.

When the time of Pilgrimage came again, Mohammed went secretly to meet the men of Yathrib. It had been agreed that they should meet at a place called Al-Akabah in a narrow glen over-shadowed by high hills. Al-Akabah means The Steep, or the Mountain Road, and is situated to the north of Meccah, a little way off the caravan road to Yathrib.

How much depended on this interview! If the new converts should fail, a year would have been passed in vain expectations, and where could another refuge for the faith be found if the people of Yathrib should refuse to welcome the new doctrines! Then, however, Mohammed reached the appointed spot, he found twelve men of the Aus and the Khazraj tribes awaiting him. They reported well on the state of feeling towards Islam in Yathrib, and promised to do all in their power to spread the faith; it was agreed that they should meet the Prophet again the following year, at the same spot, to give an account of their progress.

Before the parties separated, the twelve men of Yathrib pledged their faith to Islam, solemnly promising to worship none but the one True God, to lead pure and virtuous lives, and obey the Prophet in all that was right. This was the First Pledge of Al-Akabah, or The Steep. It was afterwards called the "Women's Pledge," because there was no mention of fighting for the cause, and the profession of faith was the same as that made by women on joining Islam.

When we think of the great power of the Mohammedans in after years, it is interesting to call to mind this early profession of faith, made by the twelve devoted believers in the depths of a ravine where they were forced to hide for fear of discovery by their enemies.

When the new converts returned to Yathrib, Mohammed sent with them a young man named Musab, to teach them the doctrines of the Koran, and to lead them in their prayers. Musab, at one time known as the best-dressed man in Meccah, was a great grandson of Hashim, but his mother and her tribe were so bitterly opposed to the Prophet that his conversion to Islam was, at first, kept secret. When it became known, Musab was disowned by his mother and her family, and was forced to fly, with the first emigrants, to Abyssinia. On his return he appeared so changed by the hardships he had undergone that his mother had no longer the heart to upbraid him. Musab had but just returned from his exile when he was sent, as missionary, to Yathrib. In course of time other teachers were sent, and among them was Abdallah, the blind man of whom we have already heard.

In patience, and with a faith that never wavered, Mohammed awaited the next meeting with the men of Yathrib. He was encouraged, from time to time, by good accounts of the spread of the faith in the new city, for the band of believers was daily increasing. When the sacred month came round, Musab, who accompanied the Moslems to Meccah, sought out the Prophet to tell him the joyful news that a large company of the Faithful were waiting to meet him in the glen of Al-Akabah. The converts of Yathrib were now sufficiently numerous to invite the Prophet to come to their city and make it his home.

For fear of arousing the suspicions of the Kuraysh, it was arranged that the meeting in the glen should take place at midnight. The utmost secrecy was observed, and the Prophet was to be accompanied only by his uncle Abbas. Abbas was not, at this time, a believer, but, being anxious for his nephew's safety, he gave him his support on this occasion.

When night had descended, and the sounds of the city were hushed, the Moslems of Yathrib left their encampments, singly, or by twos and threes, so as not to attract attention, and crept cautiously along the stony valley towards the appointed place of meeting. The Prophet and his uncle were there before them, waiting in the dark shadow of the hill. When all had assembled there were seventy-three men and two women, the twelve who had been present at the First Pledge of Akabah, the year before, being among the number.

Having enjoined silence, for fear of spies, Abbas now stood forward and addressed the assembly in a low voice. He besought the men of Yathrib to consider well before they invited his kinsman to their city, and not to deceive him by promising him protection unless they felt confident of being able to fulfil their promise; for his own clan, said Abbas, whether believers or no, would defend Mohammed from his enemies; "but," he added in conclusion, "if ye have counted the cost, and are resolved, so be it."

An aged chief of Yathrib, called Abu Bara, now came forward. "We are resolved," he said, "and will defend the Prophet with our lives."

Mohammed himself then addressed the assembly. Speaking of the blessings of Islam, he called upon all to join the cause and renounce idolatry. He would be content, he said, if the citizens of Yathrib would bind themselves to defend him and his followers as they would their own wives and children. This the "Seventy" were eager to do, and each man came forward in turn, and struck his hand on that of the Prophet in token of his oath; having repeated the words of the First Pledge, he bound himself, in addition, to defend the Prophet with his life.

One is filled with wonder at the enthusiasm inspired by Mohammed in the hearts of these early believers. Not by the promise of worldly gain, for the Moslems were, as yet, despised and oppressed, did the Prophet secure the devotion of those he converted to the faith of Islam; they must stake their all, and if they perished in the struggle, the joys of Paradise would be their reward.

The night was far advanced, and the assembly about to break up, when the silence was startled by a strange and piercing cry. Some said they were discovered by the spies of the Kuraysh, but Mohammed said it was the demon of Al-Akabah, the enemy of God, who sought to frustrate their schemes. Once again, at the battle of Uhud, were the Faithful to be scared by the voice of the Demon of Al-Akabah, crying, "Mohammed has fallen!"

Whatever was the explanation of that cry, it had the effect of hastily dispersing the assembly, and all hurried back to their several encampments as quickly as possible. Thus was achieved the Second or Great Pledge of Al-Akabah.

But in spite of all precautions, the Kuraysh got wind of the midnight meeting, and the following day, being the last of the Pilgrimage, they pursued the caravan returning to Yathrib; they only succeeded, however, in capturing one convert, whose hands they tied behind him, and they dragged him by his long hair back to Mecca. It required a good deal of courage to profess Mohammedanism in those early days, and the life of the convert was not one of ease and comfort.

After the Great Pledge of Al-Akabah the Kuraysh renewed their persecutions with so much severity that Mohammed advised all Moslems who could do so to fly to Yathrib.

Some were captured and imprisoned by the Kuraysh, but all who were free to go left the city. They locked up their houses and went quietly away, some of the streets being entirely deserted. For two months the emigration continued until none were left (except those who were imprisoned), but Mohammed and Abu Bakr with their families and Ali. These still remained—alone in the hostile city.

The Flight from Meccah

The Kuraysh were determined to rid themselves of their enemy. The governor of the city was at this time, Abu Sufyan; he was one of the Prophet's bitterest opponents, and was resolved to put an end to the conditions which, for nearly twelve years, had been constantly threatening the peace of Meccah. Though Abu Bakr was daily urging Mohammed to leave the city, he still lingered on, for, as he said, the time for flight had not yet come.

The elders of the Kuraysh now met in council, to consider the best course to pursue. Some advised banishing Mohammed, but it was objected that he might be more dangerous removed from Meccah and surrounded by his followers. Others counselled imprisonment, but this would lead to disturbances, as the friends of the Prophet would be certain to try and rescue him. When all ways had been discussed, the Kuraysh came to the conclusion that the only safe course was to put Mohammed to death. There was one objection to this; the Arabs had a system of blood revenge, and if a man was murdered, his whole clan was involved in war with the clan of the murderer; this often led to far-reaching feuds among the tribes. To prevent such a catastrophe, the Kuraysh hit on a cunning and wicked plot. A man was chosen from each clan of the tribe, including that of Hashim, Mohammed's own clan. These men were to waylay the Prophet, and all, at the same moment, to stab him with their swords. Thus it would never be known who was guilty of his blood, and the clan of Hashim would surely never dare to make war on the whole tribe.

One evening, just as it was getting dark, the conspirators concealed themselves near the Prophet's house, intending to fall on him when he came out in the early morning. But rumours of the plot having reached Mohammed, he escaped from the back of his house, and took refuge with his friend Abu Bakr. Meanwhile Ali laid himself down on the Prophet's bed, wrapped in his green mantle, to deceive any of the enemy who might chance to look in, thus allowing Mohammed time to get safely away. It was not till morning that the assassins discovered their prey had escaped.

Abu Bakr was rejoiced when Mohammed came to his house ready for immediate flight. With the wisdom and forethought which distinguished him, he had, for some time, been preparing for this event. He had bought two swift camels, which stood ready in the yard of his house, and had hired a guide who knew all the byways of the road to Yathrib; nothing was forgotten, and sufficient money for a journey had been provided.

But the Kuraysh would be certain to conclude that the Prophet had fled to Yathrib, where all his friends had already gone. With the instincts of the sons of the desert, Mohammed and his companion decided to avoid the roads most likely to be searched, and, going in another direction, to remain for some days in hiding. So they made their way cautiously, under cover of the darkness, to one of the southern suburbs, and managed to get out of the city unobserved. Still going south, they crossed a rough and stony tract of country, until they arrived at the foot of Mount Thaur, a high mountain about an hour and a half's journey from Meccah. The side of Mount Thaur is rocky and precipitous, and must have been difficult to climb in the darkness; but those who are flying for their lives are not easily hindered, and the Prophet and his companion accomplished the ascent in safety. Near the summit of Mount Thaur is a deep cave with a very narrow entrance, and here the fugitives took shelter. For three days they remained in hiding, Abu Bakr's servant coming each day to bring them food, and to report on the doings of the Kuraysh. The latter, on discovering Mohammed's escape, had immediately sent parties to scour the country in the direction of Yathrib, but finding no trace of the Prophet's flight on the northern roads, the scouts had encircled the city, searching the recesses of the rocky hills, in any of whose caves or defiles their prey might be lurking. Discovery of the fugitives would have been well rewarded, for the Kuraysh had offered a hundred camels for the heads of Mohammed and Abu Bakr.

It must have been a time of anxious suspense for the two hiding in the cave, for they knew that their enemies were close on their track; "and what can we do if we are discovered," said Abu Bakr, whispering his fears to his companion, "for we are but two against so many!" "Nay" replied Mohammed, "there is a third, for God is with us." It is related that some of the scouts came to the very mouth of the cave, and were about to enter when they noticed a thick network of spiders' webs spun across the opening. Feeling certain that no one could have passed into the cave for a considerable time, they agreed that further search was useless.

Another legend tells that a party of armed men, ranging over Mount Thaur, came to the entrance of the cave, and behold! an acacia tree had sprung up just in front of the narrow opening, and two wild pigeons were perched on its branches. One of the men called out to his companions that no one could have got in, as a tree on which a pigeon had made her nest blocked the entrance. Mohammed, crouching within, blessed the pigeons, which had been of such service to him. To this day these birds are regarded as sacred in the territory of Meccah; flocks of them are always to be seen round the Kaabah, and no one would ever think of hurting them.

On the evening of the third day, Abu Bakr's son, Abdallah, brought tidings that the Kuraysh had, for the time, abandoned the search, persuaded that Mohammed had escaped them. The moment for flight had arrived! A longer delay would be unwise, as, at any moment, a chance wayfarer might hit on some clue leading to the discovery of the fugitives. So Abdallah was ordered to make all ready for the following night. As soon as it was dark the camels were to be brought up the mountain in charge of Abu Bakr's servant and the guide, who were to wait with them in the neighbourhood of the cave.

That last day of waiting must have seemed a very long one! After dusk, Abu Bakr's daughter, Asma, came to the cave, bringing provisions for the journey. All was now ready. Truly the fate of Islam hung on a slender thread the night when the Prophet stole forth from his hiding-place, a price on his head, trusting to the darkness and the speed of his camel to be delivered from his enemies!

Mohammed and the guide rode a camel called "Al-Kaswa," or the Crop-eared, and Abu Bakr took his servant with him on the other camel. Al-Kaswa came to be famous in the history of Islam, and carried the Prophet in several of his battles, and on the occasion of his last pilgrimage to Meccah—things you will hear about by-and-by.

After descending the mountain, the fugitives went westward towards the Red Sea, thus keeping clear of the outskirts of Meccah. They made all speed till dawn, when they chanced on a Bedouin encampment. The Bedouins are wandering Arabs who have no habitations but their tents, which they move from place to place, according to the season; they are the most hospitable people in the world, and always ready to entertain strangers. As Mohammed and his companions passed the camp, an Arab lady, who was sitting in front of her tent, offered them a drink of milk, for which they must have been most grateful. But those who are hunted for their lives cannot rest long, and the travellers were soon pursuing their way northward, never stopping till sundown, except for a short halt at midday.

It was the hottest time of the year, when the desert is like a fiery furnace, and the glare intolerable. Nothing that you have ever felt could be compared to the fierce and scorching heat of the desert at midsummer. But there could be no rest for the fugitives until they had left Meccah far behind, for might not the spies of the Kuraysh be even now on their track! Avoiding the caravan roads, they made their way over rough hills, across dry river beds and hollows, for the desert has its hills and valleys just as much as the fertile country. Many miles had been covered on this first day of the Flight, and towards evening, the travellers, thinking themselves safe from pursuit, joined the caravan road between Meccah and Yathrib. They had not gone far along this road before they were aware of a horseman galloping furiously towards them. He proved to be one of the scouts of the Kuraysh returning to Meccah; but, being single-handed against four, he was unable to stop the fugitives, and even promised not to betray them if allowed to go on his way in peace.

Later on the travellers met a small caravan belonging to Talhah, a cousin of Abu Bakr. He was coming from Syria, and had, among his merchandise, some garments made of fine white cloth; of these he gave one to his cousin and one to the Prophet, whom he rejoiced to see out of reach of his enemies.

The distance from Meccah to Yathrib is roughly the same as it is from London to Edinburgh, but travelling is slow and difficult between the Arabian cities, and caravans usually take eleven days to do the journey. Mohammed and his companions had made such speed that on the morning of the eighth day they beheld, from the summit of a mountain range, the gardens and palm groves of Yathrib.

How beautiful must the tender green of the date palms have appeared to the eyes of the weary travellers! After all the hardships of the flight—the burning heat, the thirst, the want of sleep, and the haunting fear of pursuit—here, at last, was salvation in sight!

The arrival of the Prophet had long been looked for by the Moslems of Yathrib, some of whom went every day to the summit of a hill, hoping to catch sight of the fugitives. "How long!" they exclaimed, "shall the Prophet of the Lord be left to wander about, in fear of his life!" Day after day the watchers had returned, disappointed, to the city; but, at length, a Jew who was stationed on a watch-tower spied the two camels descending the opposite line of hills, and following the road leading to Kuba, a village about three miles from Yathrib. The joyful news spread fast, and when Mohammed dismounted from his camel in the shady palm groves of Kuba he found, many of his friends already waiting to receive him.

It was a charming spot, this village nestling among fruitful orchards, and shadowed by feathery date palms; to none is the sight of verdure and running water so grateful as to those who have known the privations of the desert.

Mohammed waited at Kuba for the arrival of Ali, his faithful cousin, who had risked his own life to facilitate the Prophet's escape. Great was Mohammed's joy when, on the third day, Ali arrived, having travelled from Meccah on foot.

Thus was accomplished The Flight, that great event in the history of Islam, and the Prophet of Arabia was safe among his friends. From the

Hijrah, or Flight, of the Prophet the Mohammedans date their calendar. The word Hijrah means, in Arabic, Flight. The year 1 of the Hijrah is therefore the year in which Mohammed fled from Meccah. This event happened in the year 622 of the Christian era.

The City of the Prophet

The city in which Mohammed took refuge was formerly known as Yathrib, but when the Prophet honoured this city by making it his home, it received a new name—Medinah al-Nabi, the City of the Prophet, or shortly, Medinah which means, in Arabic, The City. So in future we will make use of the new name.

As soon as it became known that the Prophet was staying at Kuba, many of the inhabitants of Medinah went out to welcome him and invite him to enter their city. It was on Friday morning, four days after his arrival, that Mohammed mounted his camel, Al-Kaswa, and passed along the shady palm groves toward his new home. Many of the chiefs of Medinah had come out to escort him, and large crowds had collected to see the new Prophet about whom so much had been heard. The people of the East wear bright and beautiful colours—deep blues and orange and flaming crimson—so a crowd has a very different appearance from one you may see in a Western town, where so many people are dressed in black or grey. Some of the chiefs wore armour, which glittered in the sunlight, and the procession had a very festive appearance, more like the escort of a conqueror than an exile.

About midday, the hour of prayer, the procession halted, and Mohammed led the prayers and preached to the assembled people. On the spot where this happened there is now a mosque, which is known as the "Friday Mosque." Friday was chosen, later on, as the day to be specially set apart for the service of God, like the Christian Sunday.

As Mohammed entered Medinah, he was beset on all sides by the invitations of the Faithful, pressing him to alight and enter their houses. Some of the people seized Al-Kaswa's bridle, so anxious were they to give the Prophet a home and a resting-place. But Mohammed, perhaps fearing to create jealousies by favouring one more than another, said: "The camel shall decide, let her go free," and leaving the rein loose on

Al-Kaswa's neck, he allowed her to take her own course. Presently she turned towards the eastern part of the town, and came into an open space; here she knelt down, stretched her neck out on the ground and refused to go further. Mohammed, accepting the sign, dismounted. "This is the place, if the Lord please!" he exclaimed. On the spot where Al-Kaswa knelt now stands the pulpit of the Prophet's mosque. But in the days of which we are speaking this piece of ground was rough and neglected. Part of it had once been used as a burying-place, and it was over-grown with thorn bushes and covered with rubbish. It belonged to two brothers, from whom Mohammed bought it as a site for the mosque he intended to build.

Soon after his arrival in Medinah, Mohammed was joined by his wife; Sauda, and his two youngest daughters, Fatimah and Umm Kulthum. They travelled from Meccah with Abu Bakr's family, and the Kuraysh had allowed them to leave the city unmolested. The Prophet's second daughter, Rukayyah, who had been one of the emigrants to Abyssinia, was already in Medinah, with her husband Othman.

The first great task to be undertaken was the building of the house of prayer or mosque, and in this work all the Moslems joined. There were many exiles from Meccah, who had fled from the persecutions of the Kuraysh; these were known as the Muhajirin or Refugees, while the citizens of Medinah, who were converts, were called Ansars, or Helpers. But as these Arabic words may be hard to remember, we will use the English ones—Refugees and Helpers. All these now joined together to assist in the work of building. The ground was leveled and the thorn bushes and rubbish cleared away; the few palm trees which grew on one side of the enclosure were cut down and their trunks used as pillars to support the roof of the mosque, which was thatched with palm leaves. The walls were made of rough stone and unbaked bricks. It was a very simple building—in later years it was enlarged and beautified, and at the present day a magnificent mosque covers the spot where Mohammed put up the first humble house of prayer, where he spent the later years of his life, and where he died and was buried.

As the labourers worked they sang a chant—sad and monotonous, as Eastern tunes usually sound to Western ears. The words they sang were these:

"O Lord there is no happiness but in Paradise,

Then have mercy on the Helpers and the Refugees!"

Mohammed joined in the chant, while he worked with his own hands. In six or seven months the mosque was finished, and Islam now possessed a house of prayer where all the Faithful could assemble in peace. Little did the builders of this first mosque realize how in a few hundred years the domes and minarets of Islam would be seen in every land of the East, and even on the far-off shores of the Atlantic! When we enter the splendid mosques of India or Constantinople, with pavements of marble or mosaic, and walls inwrought with precious stones, we are reminded of the earnest faith of those early builders, who, with mud bricks and rough pieces of unhewn stone, raised the walls of the first Moslem house of prayer. There was no ornament or decoration about the Prophet's mosque; it was in much later years that the beautiful geometrical patterns which we call Arabesques came into use. These take the place of paintings; never, in any mosque, will you see pictures or images, for the Prophet forbade his followers to make graven images or the likeness of anything in heaven or earth.

Perhaps no religion has laid greater stress on the duty of prayer than Islam. "Be constant at prayer," said the Prophet, "for prayer preserveth a man from crimes ... and the remembering of God is surely a most important duty." Mohammed enjoined his followers to pray live trines a day. 1. Before sunrise. 2. When the sun has begun to decline. 3. In the afternoon. 4. A little after sunset. 5. At night fall. These are the regular hours of prayer to be observed by all good Moslems, but many follow the example of their Prophet, and pray at other times as well. For it is written, "Celebrate the praises of thy Lord what time thou risest, and in the night and at the fading of the stars."

After a time, the question arose as to the way in which the Faithful should be summoned to prayer. The Jews blew trumpets before their synagogues, the early Christians used wooden mallets which were struck on sounding boards of wood or iron, but neither of these methods was adopted. After some discussion it was decided that the hours of prayer should be announced by a crier, or muezzin, which is the Arabic for *crier*. The first muezzin of Islam was Bilal the Abyssinian slave, who had so bravely endured the persecutions of the Kuraysh. Bilal had a very powerful voice, which fitted him well for the post of muezzin. Taking his stand on the roof of a high house near the mosque, he called the Faithful to prayer in the following words: "God is great, there is no god but the Lord. Mohammed is the Apostle of God. Come unto prayer, come unto salvation. God is great, there is no god but the Lord!" Before the early morning prayer he added, "Prayer is better than sleep."

When you visit Eastern countries you will notice the tall slender towers which are attached to almost every mosque. These are called minarets. This name is derived from an Arabic word meaning lighthouse, as the form of these towers was copied from that of the ancient lighthouse of Alexandria. Inside the minaret is a staircase leading up to a small gallery which has openings to the north, south, east and west. It is here that the muezzin stands to announce the hours of prayer. The sound of the slow, monotonous chant is heard from a great distance as he calls the Faithful to prayer in the very same words as those used by Bilal in the earliest days of Islam.

It is not necessary that a man should always enter a mosque to pray—prayers may be said anywhere. Thus, you may often see a Moslem praying in the street, in the desert, in a railway station, or in any place where he may happen to be at the time appointed for prayer.

When the mosque of Medinah was finished, Mohammed built two houses, or huts, adjoining its eastern wall and opening into the courtyard. These huts, built of mud bricks, were for the Prophet's wife, Sauda, and for the bride he was about to marry. It has always been the custom among Eastern nations (as it was among the Jews) for a man to have more than one wife. Mohammed's new bride, Ayesha, the daughter of Abu Bakr, was very beautiful. She was also witty and amusing in her conversation, and though but a child at the time of her marriage, she completely won the Prophet's affections, and remained his favourite wife to the end of his days. So young was Ayesha when she became the Prophet's wife that he used sometimes to amuse her by running races with her. Their wedding was celebrated in most simple style, the marriage feast consisting of milk. Indeed, the Prophet's household was always simple and frugal; even when he had attained to great power he never lived in a palace surrounded by pomp and splendour. He mended his own shoes and clothes, milked his goats, and often helped his wives with their household work. The Prophet's bed was a leather mattress, stuffed with palm leaves, which was laid on the floor, and his food was usually dates and barley bread, and sometimes milk and honey were added as a luxury. He gave so generously to the poor that he had little Taft for his own needs. Ayesha, speaking of this time in after years, said that the Prophet's family were often without a fire to cook by, and seldom tasted meat unless it was sent by friends.

During the early days of their residence in Medinah, the Refugees suffered many hardships. They were miserably poor, for, having forsaken their homes and occupations in Meccah, they found it hard to make a living. Abu Bakr, once a great merchant, sold clothes in the bazaar. Othman, the Prophet's son-in-law, became a fruit seller, and all tried their best to earn sufficient for their daily needs. The Helpers did what they could for their poorer brethren; they would often, seeing his face pinched with hunger, invite the Prophet to a meal, or send him a present of food. But Mohammed always shared any food that was given him with the "people of the Shed," as the poorest of the Refugees were called, who had no other shelter than a shed in the courtyard of the mosque.

Besides their struggle with poverty, the Refugees had another severe trial to undergo, for they were seriously affected by the change of climate, and suffered from violent attacks of fever. The valley of Meccah is hot and sultry, while Medinah, standing on the edge of a high tableland, is exposed to bitter east winds and storms. Rainy weather prevails during half the year, and the outskirts of the city are often flooded. The winters are intensely cold, and Mohammed once declared that "he who patiently endures the cold of Medinah and the heat of Meccah merits a reward in Paradise." No wonder that the Refugees should have felt the great change of climate; at one time there were so many who were suffering from the effects of fever that Mohammed was almost the only one able to stand up during the prayers. It speaks well for the Prophet's sincerity that his followers were willing to undergo such hardships, for no man could have inspired so strong a faith in others who was not himself a firm believer in the cause he preached.

Every Friday there was a special service in the mosque, and many came to hear the Prophet's weekly sermon. Let us try to picture one of these early gatherings of Islam. People of various races and creeds are seen in the rough building thatched with palm leaves; for besides the Refugees and Helpers, who have sworn allegiance to their faith, there are Jews, moved by curiosity to hear the "new Prophet" whose teaching so disturbed the peace of Meccah; also black Abyssinians, Persians from Irak, and perhaps a few Christian Arabs from Syria and Palestine. Above the din of the city streets is heard Bilal's far-reaching cry, "Allah hu Akbar— God is great. There is no god but the Lord. Come unto prayer, come unto salvation." When all have assembled, the Prophet enters with the salutation common among Moslems, "Peace be with you." During the prayers he stands with his back to the people facing Meccah; and his followers, standing behind him in rows, repeat the prayers, kneeling and bowing themselves to the ground, in exact imitation of their Prophet.

Before the pulpit was made, Mohammed used to stand leaning against a post while he preached the sermon. Some of his sermons have been handed down by tradition; there is one on charity, which contains the following parable: "When God created the earth, he placed mountains on it to make it firm. And the angels asked, 'O God, is there anything in Thy creation stronger than mountains?' God replied, 'Yes, iron is stronger than mountains, for it breaks them!' 'And is there anything stronger than iron?' 'Yes, fire is stronger than iron, for it melts it!' 'Is there anything in Thy creation stronger than fire?' 'Yes, water, for it quenches fire.' 'Is there anything stronger than water?' 'Yes, wind, for it overcomes water, and puts it in motion.' 'O our Sustainer,' said the angels, 'is there anything in Thy creation stronger than wind?' And God answered, 'Yes, a good man giving alms, if he give with his right hand, and conceal it from his left, for he overcomes all things!'"

By charity Mohammed understood all good actions towards one's fellow creatures, such as helping the blind, removing stones and thorns from the road, giving water to the thirsty; in fact, any kind act. Kindness of speech was also insisted on; when Mohammed was once asked by a new convert for some special rule as a guide to conduct, he replied, "Speak evil of no man." "From that time," said the convert, "I never abused anyone, whether freeman or slave." But the Prophet did not only teach charity towards one's fellow-creatures, he regarded kindness to animals as an important duty, for they are, as we read in the Koran, "a people like unto yourselves." Camels and other beasts of burden were not to be ill-used. "Fear God in respect of animals," said the Prophet; "ride them when they are fit to be ridden, and get off them when they are tired." One day a man brought him some young birds which he had caught in a wood, while their mother had fluttered round in despair at being robbed of her young. Mohammed told the man to take the birds back to the place where he had found them, and to let their mother be with them. In speaking of the kind treatment of animals Mohammed once told a story about a woman who found a dog nearly dying of thirst near a well. She had been a wicked woman, but she had compassion on the poor dog, and taking of her boot, she tied it to the end of her garment, and let it down the well to get water for the dog. For this act of kindness, said the Prophet, the woman's sins were forgiven.

It seems a wonderful thing that Mohammed, born of a fierce and warlike race, a people given to many cruel practices, should have had so much regard for compassion. He thanked God who had put it into men's hearts to be compassionate to one another, for what a terrible world it would be, said the Prophet, if men had no compassion in their hearts. Of all qualities he regarded compassion as the most God-like, and every chapter of the Koran, except one, begins with this invocation, "In the name of God, the Compassionate, the Merciful."

Mohammed as a Lawgiver

Medinah had been in a very disturbed state for many years; there were so many rival parties that it was impossible to establish a settled government, and the feuds and jealousies between the two chief tribes, the Aus and the Khazraj, were always threatening to plunge the city into war. But now that so many of the members of these tribes had sworn allegiance to Mohammed, their old quarrels were almost forgotten, and if any dispute arose, it was referred to the Prophet's decision. Thus it came to pass that, besides directing his followers in religious matters, Mohammed came to act as their judge and lawgiver. .Owing to the unsettled state of Medinah, it required both wisdom and firmness to administer justice, but Mohammed was equal to the task; and when, as time went on, he showed himself to possess all the qualities of a statesman, his power increased, and he was obeyed by his followers as though he had been a king.

A great many Jews had settled in Medinah when they had been driven from their own country by foreign invaders. They dwelt chiefly in the suburbs of the city, where they owned several fortresses and strongholds. Being very rich, they had, at times, attained great power, and oppressed their fellow-citizens, while frequent disputes had arisen between the Jewish and Arab tribes.

When Mohammed first came to Medinah, he did his best to win over the Jews, and persuade them to recognize him as a Prophet. For he believed in the Jewish scriptures, and looked upon himself as one who followed in the footsteps of the prophets of old, in preaching the worship of the True God, and denouncing idolatry. Mohammed spoke of the Jews as the "People of the Book," meaning that they possessed in their scriptures the word of God, unlike the pagan Arabs, who had no written revelations. The same title was given to the Christians, and Mohammed deeply reverenced the name of Christ, and regarded him as the greatest of the prophets who had gone before him.

Several of the institutions of the early days of Islam were taken from the Jewish religion. When the Jews prayed they turned towards Jerusalem, and for the first few months after his arrival in Medinah, the Prophet followed their example. Later on he changed the direction of prayer, and bade his followers turn towards the Kaabah of Meccah, the ancient shrine of Arabia, rendered doubly sacred by its association with the Patriarch Abraham. For Abraham, so we are told by the Arab historians, rebuilt the holy Kaabah with the help of his son Ishmael. In the earliest mosques there was a large block of stone to mark the direction of Meccah, so that the Faithful might know which way to turn their faces when they prayed. In later years the direction of prayer, or the Kiblah, was shown by a niche in the wall. Every mosque contains such a niche or recess, often beautifully decorated, and inlaid with precious stones. At the present day there are millions of pious Moslems who turn, at the hour of prayer, towards the spot they hold to be the most sacred on earth—the ancient Kaabah of Meccah.

When the Moslems first settled in Medinah they were ordered to observe the Fast of the Atonement, but the following year the Prophet instituted the Fast of Ramadan in place of the Jewish Fast. Mohammed did his best to conciliate the Jews, and not long after his arrival in Medinah, he made a treaty with them. In this charter it was laid down that the Jews should be considered as one people with the Believers. They were, however, given full liberty to practise their own religion. "The Jews will profess their religion, the Moslems theirs." If Medinah should be threatened by an enemy, the two parties must combine in the defence of the city. No one was to join the Kuraysh or their allies, for the men of Medinah were bound together against all enemies of the State. For a time the Jews remained on friendly terms with Mohammed, but they grew jealous of the increasing power of the Moslems, and in the end came to be some of the Prophet's bitterest enemies. There was yet a third party in Medinah, consisting of those who wished to be on the winning side, who, as we say, ran with the hare and hunted with the hounds. These men had not the courage to throw in their lot with the

Moslems, yet they dared not oppose them; holding, therefore, a middle course, they sometimes sided with the Prophet, and sometimes plotted against him. Mohammed had a great contempt for the Hypocrites, as these half-hearted men came to be called; he denounces them in the Koran when he says, that those who profess a religion with their lips, but deny it in their hearts, shall suffer in the lowest hell. There were thus three distinct parties in Medinah, consisting of the Moslems, the Jews, and the Hypocrites, and it must often have been very difficult to keep the peace between them.

During the first two years of Mohammed's residence in Medinah he made many of the regulations which are still observed by his followers. These are laid down in the chapters of the Koran, which were written at this time. You must not suppose that the Koran was written as a complete book. From the day that he beheld the vision of the angel on Mount Hira, almost to the day of his death, Mohammed continued writing or dictating his book, bit by bit, as occasion required. The contents of the Koran are very varied; some of the chapters are short, prophetic utterances, full of beauty and poetry, while others contain long explanations of the duties of the Believers and their relations towards each other. Writing materials were not common in Arabia in the seventh century, and the chapters of the Koran were often written on palm leaves, strips of leather, shoulder blades of sheep, in fact, on anything that came to hand. The chapters were not arranged in any regular order until after the Prophet's death.

I have mentioned the Fast of Ramadan. Ramadan is the name of the ninth month of the Arabian year, and the Prophet ordained that during this month his followers were to fast, neither eating nor drinking, from early dawn to sunset. Some say that Ramadan was observed as a fasting month by the ancient Arabs; this is quite likely, as Mohammed preserved many of the old customs of his countrymen which were not in any way connected with idolatry. The months of the Arabian year are lunar months, that is to say, they correspond with the changes of the moon, and a year composed of twelve lunar months is shorter than our solar year. Therefore the Arabian New Year does not always fall during the same season, like our New Year's Day, and in course of time those months which are regarded as summer months will become winter months, and vice versa. When Ramadan falls in the summer, it comes very hard on the inhabitants of hot countries like India, for during the whole of the day no drop of water may pass the lips of the pious Moslem.

Among the rules made by the Prophet was that forbidding the use of wine. The idolatrous Arabs often indulged freely in wine, and it was on the occasion of one of the Moslems coming to prayers when he was not sober that Mohammed forbade his followers to drink any intoxicating liquor whatsoever. All games of chance, such as are played with cards or dice, were also forbidden; neither were the Moslems allowed to lend money on usury.

A great point was made of personal cleanliness; certain washings were ordered to be performed before each of the daily prayers, and for this reason you will always see a tank of water in the courtyard of a mosque. In the desert it is allowable to use and, instead of water, for cleansing purposes. When a Moslem is about to pray he spreads out a small rug on which to kneel, for not only his person, but everything he touches during the performance of prayer must be clean and spotless. The cleansing of the teeth is also mentioned in the Koran as a necessary duty, and every Moslem must be provided with a tooth-stick.

Of all the duties of a Moslem, alms-giving is one of the most important. True charity is attained, said the Prophet, when a man gives away his favourite possession. Some devout men, as for instance, Abu Bakr, gave away almost all they had.

During the first six months following the emigration to Medinah the Prophet and his followers had been undisturbed by any fears of attack on the part of their old enemies, the Kuraysh. But these peaceful conditions were not destined to last long. The Kuraysh had dealings with the Jews of Medinah, and the latter, though they had entered into treaty with the Prophet, supplied his enemies with information as to the numbers and strength of the Moslems. About this time the Meccans began to send armed escorts with their Syrian caravans. The Prophet, on his part, gradually assumed a more warlike attitude towards his old oppressors.

In the early days of his preaching he had enjoined his followers to bear the reproaches of their enemies with meekness and patience, but, as time went on and persecutions increased, a spirit of resistance began to show itself. Even before leaving Meccah, Mohammed had announced in the Koran that permission was granted the Moslems to take up arms against the unbelievers for their unjust persecutions, and for turning the people out of their houses for no other reason than because they said, Our Lord is God.

When we condemn the Prophet for using the sword in defence of his cause, we must remember the circumstances in which he was placed. Born of a race of warriors, his forefathers had, for many generations, been accustomed to look to the sword as a means of guarding their rights. There was no settled government in Arabia, and the tribes usually took the law into their own hands, so that most disputes were finally settled by the sword. We must also bear in mind that it was on account of the cruel persecutions of the Kuraysh that the Refugees were living as exiles in a strange city, suffering poverty and hardships, their homes having been broken up. One can scarcely wonder, therefore, that Mohammed, finding himself surrounded by an ever-increasing band of followers, ready to obey him even to laying down their lives, should have made use of the means of punishing his enemies. The time had come for the fulfilment of the threats pronounced against the Kuraysh that vengeance would overtake them for their obstinate refusal to listen to the Prophet's warnings, and for their oppression of the true Believers.

It was about seven months after his arrival in Medinah that Mohammed despatched his first expedition against the Meccans. A small band, consisting of thirty Refugees, set out under the leadership of Hamzah, the Prophet's uncle, to waylay a caravan returning from Syria. This caravan, in the charge of Mohammed's enemy, Abu Jahl, was guarded by three hundred men of the Kuraysh. In the end, however, no fighting took place, as a Bedouin chief, who was friendly to both sides, interposed, and persuaded the parties to part peacefully. Not long after, several more expeditions were undertaken, three of them being led by Mohammed himself; but either they were wrongly timed and the hostile parties never met, or the caravans were too strongly guarded to be attacked. At last, however, blood was spilt, a man of the Kuraysh was killed, while two others were carried to Medinah as prisoners. These were afterwards ransomed, but one of them chose to remain at Medinah and became a convert to Islam.

After this affair, the Moslems and the people of Meccah seem to have agreed that their differences could only be settled by the sword. It was about this time that the Prophet told his followers that it was their duty to fight against the idolaters as the enemies of God.

Although we believe that religion should teach us peace, and not war, yet we cannot but admire the zeal of these early Moslems, who were ready to give their lives, their property and all they had, in the cause of their faith. Compared with their enemies, they were but a handful of men, yet Mohammed confidently told them that victory would be theirs, and that those who fell in the cause of God would be rewarded in Paradise.

At first the Believers fought for their very existence, for, beset on all sides by treachery, if they had not shown a bold front, they must have been overpowered by their enemies, who so greatly outnumbered them. Afterward war was directed against the unbelievers, that idolatry might be rooted out, and the worship of the True God be established on the earth. And, indeed, idolatry and Islam could scarcely have existed side by side, for what had they in common? With Judaism and Christianity Islam has many points of agreement, but none with the worshippers of idols. The following verses of the Koran were written at about this time: "Fight for the religion of God against those who fight against you, but transgress not by attacking them first." "Fight, therefore, until there be no temptation to idolatry, and the religion be God's alone. And if they leave off then let there be no hostility, except against the oppressors." "War is ordained for you, even though it be burdensome to you."

However mistaken he may have been, Mohammed was firmly convinced that the Believers were commanded, like the Israelites of old, to take up arms against the idolaters, and to subdue those who refused to acknowledge the True God.

The Day of Deliverance

One of the great events of the year, at Meccah, was the departure of the Syrian caravan. A regular service of caravans had been instituted by Hashim, the Prophet's great-grandfather, for Meccah was an important centre of trade and exported much valuable merchandise. Leather was one of the chief articles of the Meccan trade; this was exchanged for silks, and other costly goods, in the markets of Syria and Irak, and occasionally the Meccan caravans travelled as far as Egypt and Mesopotamia. Not only the rich merchants but almost every citizen of Meccah sent goods to these distant markets, so that the whole city was concerned for the safety of a caravan and much anxiety was felt if its return was delayed.

In the autumn of the year 623 the great Syrian caravan set out in the charge of Abu Sufyan, one of the chiefs of the tribe of Kuraysh. Abu Sufyan was a relentless opponent of Islam, and was one of those who had conspired against the Prophet's life. The caravan which he led was large and richly laden, and we can imagine the crowds that would have flocked to the outskirts of the city to watch the long string of camels winding their way up the rocky valley. When an Arab tribe is at war, its caravans are always in danger of being attacked by the enemy; great precautions were therefore taken by Abu Sufyan when nearing the territory of Medinah. But, though at one point an alarm was raised that the Moslems were in pursuit, the Syrian caravan reached its destination in safety. Three months later, in the spring of 624, this caravan was on its return journey, but while yet on the borders of Syria, Abu Sufyan was warned that his enemies were meditating an attack. He at once despatched a messenger to Meccah, to ask for help, and proceeded cautiously along a track lying near the shores of the Red Sea. On reaching a place called Badr, situated to the southwest of Medinah, Abu Sufyan went on in advance of the caravan to inquire if any strangers had been in the neighbourhood. On hearing that two men had been seen, resting their camels near a well, he carefully examined the ground, searching for any suspicious tracks. His sharp eyes, for Arabs are good scouts, soon detected some very small date stones lying by the wayside. His suspicions were at once aroused. "The spies of Mohammed have been here!" he exclaimed, as he hurried back to the caravan. You will wonder why the sight of the date stones should have put Abu Sufyan on his guard? The reason was this: the dates of Medinah are much smaller than those grown in other parts of Arabia, and, by putting two and two together, Abu Sufyan concluded that these strangers must have been spies from Medinah. Whether he guessed rightly, the sequel will show.

Meanwhile the messenger despatched by Abu Sufyan had travelled in hot haste to Meccah. Arriving before the Kaabah breathless and panting, he tore his shirt open before and behind, and sat backwards on his camel, to show that he brought bad news. The people crowded round him, and when he cried aloud, "Help, help, O Kuraysh, your caravan is pursued by Mohammed!" great excitement prevailed in the city. There was no time to be lost; an army, which was joined by almost every man of the tribe, was quickly got together, and, in the space of three days, over a thousand well-armed men marched out of Meccah, determined, once for all, to crush the power of their enemy.

We must now turn our attention to the state of things in Medinah. The time having arrived when the Syrian caravan should be on its return journey, Mohammed sent two of the Refugees to scout and get early news of its approach; as you have heard, their presence near the well at Badr was suspected by Abu Sufyan. The Prophet now called on his followers to arm themselves against the infidels, promising them rich spoil if the enterprise should succeed. But he would allow none but Moslems to go with him; some of the citizens of Medinah were eager to join the army in the hope of plunder, but Mohammed turned them back, saying, "Ye shall not go thus, believe and fight." Nearly every Refugee followed the Prophet; one of the few remaining behind was Othman, whose wife Rukayyah (Mohammed's daughter) was seriously ill. Besides the Refugees, who numbered eighty, many of the Helpers joined the little army, making in all three hundred and five men. There were seventy camels, on which the men rode in turn, but only two horses!

Mohammed marched out of Medinah with his small but determined band on the same day that the army of the Kuraysh left Meccah. This force, more than three times as large as that of the Moslems, was mounted on seven hundred camels and a hundred horses. When the Meccans were on their way to Badr they were met by another messenger bringing them news of the safety of the caravan, which had passed by another road. The leaders now consulted as to whether they should return to Meccah, or go forward and attack the Moslems. After some discussion the advice of the most warlike prevailed; the army continued its march, and on arriving at Badr encamped behind some low sand-hills.

Mohammed and his followers were also moving towards Badr when, on the third day's march, they heard of the escape of the caravan, and of the army that was advancing to meet them. The Prophet now held a council of war. Some of the Moslem leaders, as Abu Bakr and Omar, urged an immediate attack on the infidels, but Mohammed wished to give the citizens of Medinah the choice of going back if they felt so inclined, as their oath of allegiance did not bind them to fight except in defence of their own city. The Helpers, however, were all of one mind. "Prophet of the Lord," cried their leader, "march where thou wilt, make war or peace as it may please thee. I swear by the Lord who hath sent thee that we will follow thee even to the world's end; there shall none remain behind!" "Go forward then with the blessing of God," said the Prophet.

The Valley of Badr is bounded by steep hills on the north and east; from these hills a stream flows, and the lower ground is well watered by several springs and wells. When Mohammed descended into the valley he wisely occupied the ground near the springs, where he made his camp, thus gaining possession of the water. The Moslems, tired with their march, slept peacefully. A rough hut of palm branches was constructed for the Prophet and Abu Bakr, and one of the Helpers stood on guard at the entrance with a drawn sword in his hand.

It was a rough night, this night before the battle which was to decide the fate of Islam; rain fell in torrents and cold blasts of wind swept

MOHAMMED AT THE BATTLE OF BADR

across the desolate land. In the early morning Mohammed drew up his men, ordering them to stand firm and await the attack of the enemy. It was not long before the Meccans were seen advancing over the sand-hills; the slope of the ground prevented their full numbers being at once discerned, and the Moslems imagined the attacking force to be much smaller than it was in reality. But the Prophet fully realized the serious risk to which his army was exposed, and, retiring for a moment into the hut of palm branches, he thus prayed earnestly for victory; "O Lord, forget not Thy promise of help, for if this little band should perish, there will be none to offer Thee pure worship, and idolatry will prevail."

The enemy was now close at hand, but the Moslems stood firm, as they had been ordered to do. Some skirmishing took place for the possession of the wells, but fighting did not at once become general. Single combats were common in Arab warfare, and three stalwart champions stood out from the Meccan army, each challenging a Moslem to try his strength with him. Of the Moslems who eagerly came forward, one was an elderly man of about sixty-five, another a powerful warrior in the prime of life, and the third a young man who wore a white plume on his helmet as a distinguishing mark; their features, being hidden by their armour were not visible.

The Meccans now asked for the names of their opponents. "I am Hamzah, the son of Abd al-Muttalib, surnamed the 'Lion of God,'" replied the Prophet's uncle. The old man's name was Ubaidah, and the youth wearing the white plume was Ali, the son of Abu Talib and cousin of Mohammed. The champions, facing each other, attacked in deadly earnest; Hamzah and Ali each slew his man, but Ubaidah, after a severe encounter, received wounds of which he died in a few days. The two armies now engaged in a fierce struggle for victory, and prodigious deeds of valour were performed on both sides. Ali fought with no armour to his back, thus showing his resolve to conquer or die. The Arab historians tell of many a desperate deed done this bleak wintry day on the battlefield of Badr. The Prophet, moving among his men, roused their ardour by reminding them of the cause for which they fought. God was on their side, he said, and Paradise would be the reward of those who fell. The very winds of heaven seemed to assist the Moslem cause, and fierce gusts laden with blinding storms of rain swept down the valley in the face of the enemy. Gabriel with a thousand angels was sweeping as a whirlwind on the foe, said the Prophet. Another storm sped by—it was Michael and his angels coming to the help of the true Believers. And again, the Prophet said that Seraphil with a legion of angels was descending to aid the cause of God.

The issue of the battle still hung in the balance when Mohammed picked up a handful of gravel, and threw it in the direction of the enemy. "May confusion seize them!" he exclaimed. This was the turning point of the battle; whatever the cause, the Meccans now began to waver, unable any longer to withstand the fierce onsets of their opponents.

The Kuraysh, with vastly superior numbers, good arms and horses, should have had the advantage of their enemies; but the Moslems, fighting with a burning enthusiasm for their cause, and encouraged by the presence of their Prophet to deeds of bravery and self-sacrifice, gained a moral advantage, and this it was which won them the day.

The retreating army of the Kuraysh was soon in full flight; hindered by the deep sand, which was heavy with the rain of the previous night, many threw away their armour, the better to escape the pursuit of the victorious Moslems. Several of the foremost chiefs of Meccah had been slain, among them Abu Jahl, the commander of the army. In all, forty-nine Meccans lay dead, and many were taken prisoners, while the Moslems had lost only fourteen men. In their hurried flight the Kuraysh abandoned their camp, leaving rich store of plunder for the victors, who secured a hundred and fifty camels and fourteen horses, besides weapons, armour, leather goods and carpets. A dispute arose as to the division of the spoil, some of those who had distinguished themselves in the battle claiming that a larger share was due to them than to those who had stayed to guard the camp; but Mohammed decided that all should share alike. The laws laid down by the Prophet, after Badr, for the distribution of spoil taken in battle, hold good to this day among his followers. One-fifth was set aside for the cause of God—for the Prophet and his family, or for the poor and the orphan, as occasion required; the rest was equally divided among those who had taken part in the battle, an extra portion being awarded to the horsemen.

Darkness was falling when all the spoil had been collected from the enemy's camp, and it now but remained to bury the dead. Thus ended the Day of Deliverances as the eventful day of Badr came to be called. Of the seventy prisoners in the hands of the Moslems, two were executed by the Prophet's orders, one of them being a renegade from the Faith. The rest of the prisoners were taken to Medinah, and Mohammed gave those who had charge of them special injunctions to treat them with kindness and forbearance. This was contrary to the usual custom of Arab warfare, and, in after years, one of these prisoners blessed the men of Medinah who had treated them with so much consideration, giving them the best of their food, and letting them ride while they themselves walked. The prisoners were afterwards ransomed by their kinsmen in Meccah; several, who became converts to Islam, were set free without payment, and those whose relations could not afford a ransom were given their freedom on condition that they each taught ten boys of Medinah the art of writing.

As the victorious army was returning to Medinah, Zaid and another messenger were sent forward to announce the good news. Zaid, mounted on the Prophet's favourite camel, Al-Kaswa, hurried to the city, and, as the people crowded anxiously round him, cried aloud that the army of the Kuraysh had been utterly defeated, and that Abu Dahl, the sinner, was slain.

The next day Mohammed arrived, but he was met by the sorrowful news of the death of his daughter, Rukayyah, who had but just been buried when the messenger announcing the victory entered the city.

We can picture the dismay and consternation of the people of Meccah when their army returned crestfallen and defeated, many of their bravest chiefs missing, the baggage deserted and in possession of the enemy. The city was roused to a pitch of intense excitement and fury, the people vowing that they would not even mourn the dead until they had wreaked vengeance on their foe.

About three months later Abu Sufyan went forth with two hundred horsemen to pillage the country round about Medinah. He wished to make a rapid march and achieve his purpose before the citizens of Medinah could be warned. No baggage animals were taken, as they would have delayed the march, and each horseman carried a sack of meal on his saddle. In a fertile valley a few miles distant from Medinah the raiders laid waste the cornfields, and burnt the palm groves and farm houses to the ground, killing two of the farmers. Just as they were preparing to depart, the Prophet himself appeared at the head of an armed force, and the Meccans turned and fled, throwing away their meal bags to lighten the weight on their horses. The Moslems called this skirmish, derisively, the Battle of the Meal Sacks.

The Jews and those Arab tribes who were hostile to the Prophet were a constant source of annoyance to him. During the year following the Battle of Badr, the peace of Medinah was continually disturbed by disputes and revolts, and there was more than one plat against the Prophet's life. On the other hand, several of his avowed enemies were put to death by his followers, who wrongly believed they were thus serving the cause of God. Certain Jews who had insulted a Moslem woman were besieged in their fortress, and when they surrendered the whole tribe was sent into banishment.

A few days before the battle of Badr, the Prophet's daughter, Fatimah, was betrothed to Ali, and their marriage took place about three months later. Ali was about twenty years of age, and Fatimah barely fifteen. In course of time two sons were born to them, who were named Hasan and Husain; these were the only grandsons of the Prophet who survived him. In the same year Mohammed married Hafsah, who was a widow, and the daughter of Omar.

Although the Moslems had not again been molested by their enemies since the skirmish of the Meal Sacks, the Kuraysh had not forgotten their solemn vows of vengeance for their kinsmen slain at Badr. Events, destined to be of serious import to the small and harassed band of Believers, were preparing in Meccah. Of these we shall hear in the next chapter.

The Field of Uhud

The Prophet was in the mosque at Kuba, a village about two miles from Medinah, when a messenger from Meccah handed him a sealed letter. It had been sent by Abbas, the Prophet's uncle, and contained the news that an army of three thousand men was on the point of marching out of Meccah against the Moslems. Abbas, as you will remember, was not a believer, but he had always shown an interest in his nephew's welfare, and now sent him a secret message to warn him of his danger. For the army that was about to march on Medinah was a far more formidable force than that which the Moslems had defeated at Badr.

The men of Meccah, determined on vengeance, had devoted the whole profits of the Syrian caravan to fitting out their army. Messengers had been sent to the warlike Bedouin tribes, inviting them to join the enterprise, and the Kuraysh had now at their disposal over three thousand well-armed men, of whom seven hundred wore coats of mail. The cavalry consisted of two hundred picked men mounted on good horses, the rest rode camels. Some of the Meccan women accompanied the army, encouraging the warriors with their warlike songs.

As soon as Mohammed had read his uncle's letter, he hurried back to Medinah. It was in times of sudden danger that his powers of administration and resource were at their best. The town was quickly put into a state of defence, but not before the news arrived that the Meccans were encamped in the plain below Mount Uhud, a mountain three miles to the north of Medinah, and were laying waste the country, cutting down the corn as food for their horses.

A discussion now arose as to whether it were best to remain in the town, on the defensive, and await the attack of the enemy, or to go out and risk a battle in the open. Mohammed with the older and more discreet among his followers were inclined to the first alternative, but the younger men, impatient at the ravages on the cornfields, urged bolder measures. In the end their advice was taken, and the Prophet decided to lead his army out, and attack the enemy. It was Friday morning, the mosque was crowded with worshippers, and the Prophet, preaching his weekly sermon, incited the Moslems to fight bravely in the cause of Islam. The Lord would help them to victory, he said, if they remained steadfast. After the evening prayer, Mohammed put on his helmet and coat of mail and led his little army in the direction of Mount Uhud. The Moslem army consisted of barely a thousand men, and on the desertion of the leader of the Hypocrites with his three hundred followers, only seven hundred remained to do battle against a force numbering over three thousand. That night, the two armies encamped with but a ridge of black volcanic rock separating them; indeed, so near were they to each other that the Moslems could hear the neighing of the enemy's horses.

With the first glimmering of dawn, the Moslems advanced, a guide leading them by the nearest way to the mountain. Just as the rising sun tinged the black peaks of Mount Uhud, they came in sight of the enemy. It was the hour of prayer, and Bilal, raising his voice, uttered the accustomed words: "God is great, there is no god but the Lord. Mohammed is the Apostle of God. Come unto prayer, come unto salvation. God is great, there is no god but the Lord!" Led by the Prophet, the whole Moslem army bowed itself in prayer, in the very presence of the enemy. It must have been a strangely impressive sight.

Mohammed took up his position on a piece of rising ground, with the cliffs of Mount Uhud behind him. To his left the wall of rock turned, leaving an opening through which the enemy might force his way. To cover this weak point, Mohammed placed his best archers on a neighbouring hill, ordering them to stand firm at their post, whatever might be the course of the battle.

The Meccan army was disposed in three divisions, the centre being led by Abu Sufyan, while a Kuraysh named Talhah carried the banner, for his family claimed the hereditary right of bearing the standard of the tribe in battle. The left wing of the army was commanded by a son of Abu Jahl, and the right by a warrior who obtained great renown in after years. This was Khalid, a leader of dauntless courage, and the hero of many a daring exploit.

As usual in Arab warfare, fighting began with single combats. Talhah, the standard-bearer, first advanced from the ranks of the Meccan army, but he never returned, for the sword of Ali, with one blow, struck him lifeless to the ground. Talhah's brother then rushed forward and, seizing the banner, challenged the bravest of the Moslems to fight with him; but he too fell, slain by the sword of Hamzah, the "Lion of God." Three more of the family of hereditary standard-bearers fell, one after another, in single combat. The Moslem champions seemed invincible. Enraged at the loss of some of their bravest men, the Meccan leaders ordered a general attack, and the two armies engaged in a deadly struggle.

The Moslems fought with the same fierce determination that they did at Badr, and the Meccans, though vastly superior in numbers, fell back before their advance. The white plume of Ali and the ostrich feather which distinguished Hamzah were seen wherever the battle raged fiercest, and many Meccans were laid low by the swords of these two mighty warriors. In full confidence of success the Moslems broke through the enemy's lines and fell upon their camp. Perceiving this, the archers stationed on the hill could not resist the temptation to plunder, and against the direct commands of their leader, they deserted their post and joined in the pursuit of the enemy. This act of disobedience was fatal to the Moslems, for Khalid, quickly seizing his opportunity, led the Meccan horse through the now unguarded opening in the hills, and suddenly fell on the Moslems from the rear.

Thus was the tide of battle turned, and confusion seized the Moslem host. The Meccans raised their war-cry, calling on their idols Hubal and Uzza, and pressed the attack on every side. Many of the bravest Moslems fell, including Musab (the first missionary sent to Medinah), who carried the standard of the Refugees. But the heaviest loss that befell the Prophet's army on the fatal day of Uhud was that of Hamzah, the "Lion of God," who was pierced by the javelin of an Abyssinian.

Though the followers of the Prophet fought with the courage of desperation, they were at length overcome, and fell back on the fastnesses of Mount Uhud. It was in vain that Mohammed called on his panic-

stricken men to stay their flight. His words were unheeded. As the enemy swept across the plain, the Prophet was surrounded, and but for the
devotion of some of his friends, could not have escaped alive. Wounded
by an arrow, the head of which remained embedded in his face, he was
struck down by a violent blow on the head, which drove the rings of
his helmet into his cheek, and inflicted a deep gash in his forehead. His
most devoted followers (there were seven Helpers and seven Refugees)
closed around their Prophet, and with difficulty managed to convey him
to a place of safety in one of the deep recesses of the mountain.

The Meccans, seeing their enemy fall, believed him to be dead; the cry
went up "Mohammed is dead!" and the echoes of the gloomy mountain repeated "Mohammed is dead!" Terror struck the hearts of the
Believers, for in that fateful cry they heard, as they thought, the voice
of the Demon of Al-Akabah, the same who had scared the seventy
disciples in the glen three years before.

Utterly disheartened, many believing their Prophet dead, the defeated
Moslems fled before the foe, and took refuge in a deep cleft in the side
of the mountain. The whole aspect of Mount Uhud is strangely dark
and doomful; its curious and fantastic outline has an unreal look like
that of a mountain seen in a dream, while the masses of black volcanic
rock give it the appearance of a mountain of iron.

The Meccans now ranged over the field of battle and barbarous-
ly mutilated the bodies of the slain. Searching in vain for the body
of Mohammed, they began to doubt if he were truly dead, and Abu
Sufyan, approaching the foot of the mountain, called aloud the names
of Mohammed, Abu Bakr, Omar. There was silence, and Abu Sufyan
cried out, "They are dead, ye are well rid of them!" But Omar's voice
was heard in reply, "Thou enemy of God, thou liest, we will yet repay
thee for this day." "We shall meet again," Abu Sufyan said, "let it be at
Badr, in a year's time." Omar agreed, and Abu Sufyan took his departure and gave the order for the homeward march. About sundown, the
Meccans, having buried their dead, were seen moving away across the
plain, the men riding the camels and leading the horses.

When news of the defeat reached Medinah, many of the inhabitants hurried to the battlefield, and the women came out ready to attend to the wounded. The survivors were searching among the granite boulders for the killed and wounded, and there was many a sad scene as the dead were recognized, often cruelly mutilated by the enemy's hands. The ancient Arabs were in the habit of mutilating the bodies of those killed in battle, but Mohammed, greatly to his to his credit, absolutely forbade this barbarous practice among his followers.

The Moslems lost seventy men at Uhud, the same number that the Meccans lost at Badr. Among the many wounded were Abu Bakr, Ali and Omar. Fatimah, who had come to the field with Safiyyah, the Prophet's aunt, bathed and dressed her father's wounds. Safiyyah had been devoted to her brother Hamzah, and was overcome with sorrow for his loss. But when she looked on his mangled body her grief knew no bounds, and the Prophet and Fatimah stood by and sobbed aloud.

Thus the day of Uhud closed in sorrow and mourning. The women wailed for the fallen, and above all for Hamzah, the beautiful and brave who had been beloved by all. The little mosque of rough stone which in after years was built over the spot where he was buried is still visited by the pilgrims when they come to pray at the tombs of the martyrs who fell on the ill-fated field of Uhud.

The Siege of Medinah

On the day after the battle of Uhud, Mohammed led out the remnants of his defeated army to follow the movements of the Meccans, fearing they might return to attack Medinah. A banner was placed in the hands of Abi Nair, who, though still suffering from his wounds, mounted his horse, and rode in the direction of Meccah to scout for signs of the enemy. The object of this expedition was to show that if their city should be threatened, the Moslems were still able and ready to defend it. The Kuraysh had, in fact, halted and discussed the plan of an attack on Medinah, but the army was too exhausted for further efforts, and in the end it was decided to continue the homeward march. Mohammed and his small force remained in the field for five or six days, when, being satisfied that the Meccans had really departed, they returned to Medinah.

Mohammed, whose firm belief in the final triumph of Islam never seemed to waver, tried to raise the drooping spirits of his followers. It was through their disobedience to his commands, he told them, that the battle had been lost. If the archers had remained where they were posted, and resisted the temptation to plunder, victory would have been on the side of the Moslems.

There is no doubt that the defeat of Uhud had the effect of weakening the Moslem cause, just as the victory of Badr had strengthened it. Those desert tribes who were against the Prophet saw their opportunity of raiding the territory of Medinah, and several expeditions had to be despatched to protect the property of the citizens. One tribe in particular behaved in a most treacherous manner; the Prophet was asked by one of the chiefs of this tribe to send missionaries to instruct the people in the new faith, but when the missionaries arrived they were massacred almost to a man. The Jews, too, entirely disregarding their treaty, stirred up the people to revolt and laid a plot against the Prophet's life. The tribe thus suspected of treachery was ordered to quit the city, and on refusing was besieged. After the siege had lasted fifteen days the Jews submitted and agreed to emigrate. They were allowed to take all their goods with the exception of their arms. Thus, as the Prophet had told them, war was ordained for the Moslems whether they liked it or not. For their very existence they must fight continually, and it is a wonder that the hard-pressed band of Believers managed to hold their own against so many enemies.

About this time, the widow of a citizen of Medinah who had been killed at Uhud begged the Prophet to redress her wrongs. She had two daughters, but her husband's brother had taken possession of the whole inheritance, leaving nothing for the widow and her daughters. This was in accordance with the custom of the times, as, among the ancient Arabs, women did not usually inherit property. But Mohammed, recognizing the injustice of this, made a law entitling women to a share of the property left by their husbands or fathers. The exact amount of this share depended on circumstances. We often hear of the subjugation of Eastern women, but this is due more to the general idea in the East of the position of women than to any regulations made by Mohammed, for he did a great deal to improve the condition of women in Arabia, and made various laws for their benefit.

Some people are under the impression that the Mohammedans believe that a woman has no soul. This is a strange error, for the Koran expressly states that all who have faith and do good works, whether they be men or women, shall enter Paradise. There is a story told about an old woman who asked the Prophet what she should do to be able to enter Paradise. Mohammed replied that no old women would be admitted, upon which the woman wept until he explained that his meaning was that at the resurrection they would all be made young again.

You will remember that after the battle of Uhud, Abu Sufyan had challenged the Moslems to meet him at Badr in a year. When the time for this appointment drew near Mohammed appealed to his followers to arm themselves and march out with him. But many were disinclined to venture, the remembrance of Uhud being still fresh in their minds. The

THE MECCAN ATTACK ON MEDINAH

Prophet, upbraiding his men for their cowardice, swore that he would go to Badr even though none should follow him. For very shame the Moslems volunteered to go and fight, and in the end fifteen hundred men assembled. This was a larger force than Mohammed had ever led before, but when he arrived at Badr there was no enemy to fight with!

The Kuraysh had marched out of Mecca with an army of two thousand foot soldiers and fifty horsemen, but finding no pasture on the way to feed their numerous camels (the season being an unusually dry one) they had returned home.

It was the time of the annual fair at Badr, and the Moslems pitched their camp and remained there a week. From warlike enterprises they turned their thoughts to commerce, and, having exchanged their goods to advantage, returned well satisfied to Medinah. This affair was named the second Badr.

But though Abu Sufyan did not keep his appointment at Badr, he had not given up the chief aim of his life. He was still fixed in his determination to overthrow the power of Mohammed, of the exile who had left his native city a hunted fugitive, and was now as a king with an army of devoted followers at his beck and call.

Abu Sufyan took some time to mature his plans, and it was not till the spring of A.D. 627, two years after the battle of Uhud, that he was ready to march out of Mecca at the head of ten thousand men, many of the desert tribes having joined the standard of the Kuraysh.

Terror and dismay prevailed in Medinah when news came that such an overwhelming force was approaching to besiege the city. Mohammed, who seems to have had the useful gift of being able to think quickly in an emergency, immediately prepared his plans for the defence of the town.

For the first time in Arab, warfare entrenchments were used; a Persian convert named Salman, who had been present at sieges in other countries, suggested the idea. The solid stone houses of Medinah, built closely together, made a good fortification on one side of the town, but there were large open spaces to the south and east which were quite unprotected. Along these it was proposed to dig a deep trench, and the work was begun without delay. Shovels and pick-axes were collected, as well

as baskets in which to remove the soil, for the Arabs had no wheel-bar-
rows. All the clans joined in the work, as they had done at the building
of the mosque; as the Prophet worked he sang the accustomed chant:

"O Lord, there is no happiness but in Paradise,

Then have mercy on the Helpers and the Refugees,"

while the labourers answered:

"Unto Mohammed have we pledged our faith,

To fight his foes and flee not until death."

In six days a wide and deep trench had been dug along nearly all the
unprotected parts of the town. The houses outside this trench were
deserted, and all the women and children were placed in the towers
within the town. The preparations were hardly completed when the
enemy appeared.

The new method of fortification surprised and disconcerted the
Meccans. Accustomed to use their swords in hand-to-hand fighting, they were not prepared to find a barrier placed between them and
their foes. They even said that the Moslems were acting against all the
traditions of Arab warfare and taking an unfair advantage. The effect
of archery was first tried; showers of arrows and stones from catapults
were aimed at the Moslem camp, doing, however, little damage. A sudden assault was then made at a point where the trench was narrow and
weakly defended, and a few bold horsemen put spurs to their horses and
cleared it. One of these was killed by Ali, who engaged him in single
fight, and the rest were dispersed. Thus the first day passed in fruitless
attempts to come to close quarters with the defenders of Medinah.

In the night, a council of war was held in the Meccan camp, and it
was decided to make use of the large numbers of men at the disposal of
the besiegers by surrounding the town and pressing the attack from all
sides at once. The garrison of Medinah, numbering about three thousand men, were severely tried by these methods; there were not enough
men to guard the long line of defences, and the harassed soldiers never
knew at what point the next attack would be directed. But the Moslem
outposts were so watchful that it seemed impossible to take them un-
awares. Even at night there were constant alarms; Khalid, the leader

who had secured the victory at Uhud, laid schemes to surprise the defenders, and led several gallant night attacks, but all to no purpose, and he never succeeded in crossing the trench. Another brave commander called Amr distinguished himself by several daring attempts to force a way into the town, but he, too, was unsuccessful.

In the early part of the siege, Abu Sufyan had sent envoys to the chiefs of the Jewish tribe of Kuraizah, proposing that they should break their treaty with Mohammed and join the Meccan army. The Jews, thinking that the Kuraysh and their allies must, in the end, overcome the Moslems, agreed to these proposals and went over to the enemy, thus deserting the Prophet at his greatest need, for he could ill spare any men from his already small garrison. The Kuraizah were afterwards bitterly to repent their treacherous conduct.

The besieged garrison were indeed in sore straits; the town was full of treachery, and if the enemy had succeeded in forcing the defences, the Moslem rear would have been attacked by the Jews and the Hypocrites, who were only waiting to see which way the tide turned. As we read in the Koran, "The enemy came upon them from above and from beneath; Lad the sight became confused, and hearts reached to the throats."

Getting no rest night or day, the Moslem soldiers were completely worn out, and it became absolutely necessary to divide the army in two sections so that one half of the men might sleep while the others kept watch on the defences. With the numbers on duty so reduced, the utmost alertness was required to guard against surprises. We can judge of the vigilance of the defenders of Medinah by the fact that after a siege of twenty days the Meccan army of ten thousand men had been unable to capture the city.

The leaders of the Kuraysh were disheartened at the ill-success of their enterprise; the men were suffering from the bleak and wintry weather, and the horses and camels were dying for want of forage, which was very scarce and quite insufficient for the needs of such a large army. One night a violent storm arose, piercing gusts of wind swept across the plain, and heavy rains drenched the shivering men in the Meccan camp. The wind increased to a hurricane, the camp fires were extinguished, tents were blown down, and the scene was one of wild confusion. Suddenly Abu Sufyan resolved to break up the camp and march homeward. The army, only too eager to obey his orders, hurriedly prepared for departure, while some, in their terror, spread the alarm that Mohammed had raised the storm by enchantment. When morning dawned, the Meccan host had vanished, not one of the enemy was in sight. So ended the siege of Medinah, afterwards known as the "Battle of the Ditch."

When the army of the Kuraysh dispersed, the allies returned to their respective homes, and the Jewish tribe of Kuraizah repaired to their fortress a few miles distant from Medinah. But their faithless desertion of the Moslems in their hour of need was not to remain unpunished. Mohammed, perhaps fearing the presence so near home of his avowed enemies, marched forth and besieged the Kuraizah in their stronghold. After holding out for about three weeks the Jews surrendered on condition that their punishment should be decided by a member of the tribe of Aus, with which they were allied. Mohammed agreed, and a chief of the tribe came to pronounce judgment. His sentence was terribly severe, for he condemned all the men to be executed, and the women and children to be sold as slaves. It is much to be regretted that Mohammed allowed this sentence to be carried out, although it cannot be denied that the Jews had behaved treacherously in breaking their treaty with the Prophet at a moment of such grave peril, and in joining the enemies of Medinah. The sentence of death in such cases was not unusual in olden times, though according to our present ideas it seems very severe justice.

The Pledge of the Tree

There was little rest for the Moslems during the year following the siege of Medinah. Although no important battle with the Meccans took place, we hear of numerous encounters with hostile tribes and bands of plunderers, some of whom ventured into the very outskirts of Medinah, driving off large numbers of camels. True words had the Prophet spoken when he said, "War is ordained for you, even though it be burdensome unto you." The believer in Islam must be ready to give his life for the cause, should it be required of him. Though in some cases the Prophet was severe in punishing the enemies of the Faith, there are many instances recorded of his mercy and forgiveness, and of the spirit of humanity which he tried to instill into that nation of warriors. On one occasion when despatching an expedition against a Bedouin tribe, he addressed the commander of the force in these words: "In no case shalt thou use deceit, nor shalt thou kill any child." Mohammed invariably ordered his commanders to spare the weak, and the women and children, and not to destroy the houses of the inhabitants of a conquered town. He gave a charter to the Christians, in which he undertook to protect their churches and monasteries, and granted them full liberty to practise their religion.

It was now six years since the Prophet and his followers had beheld their native city. Notwithstanding all they had suffered at the hands of their countrymen, Meccah was still dear to the hearts of the Moslems, and there were many who longed to revisit their old home. It happened about this time that Mohammed had a dream. He was in Meccah, amid the scenes of his youth and early manhood. Again, he saw the familiar streets, the overshadowing heights of Mount Abu Kubais, and in the midst of the city the dark square form of the ancient temple of Arabia— the holy Kaabah. Mohammed saw himself with a large company of his disciples performing the rites of pilgrimage, and when he awoke a great yearning for the fulfilment of his dream filled the Prophet's heart. Surely, he thought, the unbelievers would not refuse the Moslems permission to visit the holy shrine if they came unarmed as pilgrims. Many of his followers were of one mind with the Prophet, and anxious to make the attempt to visit Mecca.

You must know that the practice of making the pilgrimage to Mecca dates back to very early times. The Arabs say that Abraham instituted some of the ceremonies of pilgrimage in the days when the Kaabah was the temple of the True God; and the tribes from all parts of Arabia still continued to visit the national shrine after it had become the dwelling-place of idols. When a pilgrim enters the sacred territory of Mecca, he must wear a particular dress. The "ihram," or pilgrim's dress, consists of two straight pieces of cotton cloth, one of which is wrapped round the lower part of the body, and the other thrown over the left shoulder and knotted at the right side, thus leaving the right arm and shoulder bare. The pilgrim must have his head shaved, and no turban or other head-covering is allowed. This dress is still worn by the pilgrims of the present day.

It was during one of the sacred months that Mohammed, having put on the pilgrim's dress, mounted his camel, Al-Kaswa, and rode towards his native city. He was followed by about fifteen hundred Moslems, who brought with them the camels intended for sacrifice, which they decorated with garlands. The last ceremony of the pilgrimage is a sacrifice, in remembrance of Abraham's sacrifice of the ram, which he offered up in the place of his son.

The Kuraysh, hearing of Mohammed's approach, and not believing in his peaceful intentions, sent out an armed force to meet him.

Khalid, at the head of two hundred horsemen, galloped on in advance, ready to bar the way to the pilgrims. The Moslems were not equipped for fighting, so when Mohammed heard of these warlike preparations from one of his scouts, he turned off the main road, and followed a track leading across a rough and rocky country, to Hudaibiyah, a place about eight miles from Mecca.

The Moslems had not long halted at Hudaibiyah when they saw a

cloud of dust in the direction of the Holy City, and a party of horsemen approached. The Kuraysh had sent the chief of one of the tribes to
question Mohammed as to his intentions; the Prophet replied that he
had not come prepared for war, and only begged permission to visit the
holy Kaabah and perform the rites of pilgrimage. So the chief departed
to deliver this message to the Kuraysh. But they were not satisfied, and
presently sent another messenger to say that the people of Meccah were
greatly excited and quite determined that Mohammed should not enter
their city. Discussions continued, and messengers travelled backwards
and forwards trying to arrange some agreement between the two parties. One of these envoys, in describing his interview with Mohammed
to the leaders of the Kuraysh, said that, though he had been at the court
of the Roman Emperor in Constantinople, and had seen the Kings of
Persia and Abyssinia surrounded by pomp and magnificence, yet never
had he seen a sovereign receive such reverence and obedience from his
subjects as this Prophet received from his devoted followers.

Finally Mohammed sent his son-in-law Othman into Meccah to
try and arrange matters with the elders of the Kuraysh. The Moslems
waited impatiently to hear the result of Othman's mission; but when
three days had passed and he did not return, grave anxiety was felt
for his safety. Suddenly a report was spread that Othman had been
murdered in Meccah. Mohammed, greatly fearing treachery, gathered
his people round him, calling on them to stand by him to avenge the
death of Othman if the report should prove true. All were eager to give
their services. Mohammed was standing in the shade of an acacia tree,
and every pilgrim came to him in turn, striking his hand on that of
the Prophet as a pledge that he would stand by him to the death. The
"Pledge of the Tree" was ever after remembered by Mohammed as a
proof of the devotion of his followers.

Othman, however, returned safely, and though he had not succeeded in
his mission, he had persuaded the Kuraysh to try and make a treaty of
peace with Mohammed, and so end the state of war, which was begin-
ning to tell heavily on both sides. A chief called Suhail was sent out to
arrange the terms of the treaty. It was then agreed that war between the

Moslems and the Meccans should cease for ten years. The desert tribes were to be free to ally themselves with either side. The Moslems were to depart without entering Meccah, but permission was given them to make the pilgrimage to the Kaabah during the following year, and to remain in Meccah for three days, during which time all the inhabitants would leave the city and camp in the neighbourhood. These terms having been approved by both parties, Ali was summoned to write out the treaty at the Prophet's dictation. The witnesses, among whom were Abu Bakr, Omar and Othman, then signed their names below. A copy of this important document was made for the Kuraysh to keep, and the Prophet took the original with him to Medinah.

So ended the expedition to Hudaibiyah. Mohammed considered that he had scored a victory in the advantages gained by the terms of the treaty, but the Moslems were disappointed in their hopes of visiting their native town that year.

In the autumn following the events just related Mohammed took a very important step. Six messengers were despatched from Medinah on the same day, each one bearing a letter from the Prophet to one of the chief rulers of the world. Of these letters one was addressed to Heraclius, the Roman Emperor (at that time in Syria), one to the King of Persia, and the others to the Roman Governor of Egypt, the King of Abyssinia, and the governors of the provinces of Ghassan and Yemama. Mohammed, the Apostle of God, invited the nations of the earth to join Islam and share in its privileges. The blessings of peace would fall on those who followed his guidance. And those who refused must acknowledge the supremacy of God's Prophet by paying tribute.

Such mighty rulers as the Roman Emperor and the King of Persia must have been surprised, and perhaps amused, at the pretensions of this obscure chief of desert tribes, for so they would have regarded Mohammed. They never dreamed that before ninety years had passed these desert tribes would have become masters of Syria, Persia, and Egypt, their conquests extending along the coast of North Africa to the Straits of Gibraltar. It was the Arabs who gave Gibraltar its name, calling it Jebel-al-Tarik, or the Mount of Tarik, after the general who crossed the straits and founded the Moslem dominion in Spain. So Gibraltar bears to this day the name of one of the conquering chiefs of Islam. But we are very much anticipating events, and at the time of our story the kingdom of the Moslems only comprised the city of Medinah with some of the surrounding country.

It is unlikely that any scheme of foreign conquest could have occupied the Prophet's mind, for he had no means of carrying through any such plan. Up to this time the Moslems had barely been able to hold their own, and had but lately been besieged in their city by the allied armies of the Meccans and most of the tribes of Arabia. It seems clear, then, that the Prophet's aim in addressing the great rulers of the earth was the establishment of the religion he believed to be the true one. Not only Arabia, but the whole world should share in the blessings of Islam. Mohammed probably little dreamed to what distant lands the Faith would be carried so short a time after his death.

The Jewish tribes were still bitterly opposed to the Moslems and continually plotting against them. About a hundred miles north of Medinah lay the village of Khaibar; it was situated on the edge of a fertile oasis and strongly fortified. The Jews inhabiting this district had been suspected of planning attacks on Medinah, so, to defeat their schemes, the Prophet marched on Khaibar, and besieged its forts. The campaign lasted about two months. The Jews fought bravely in defence of their fortresses, and at one time the siege was nearly abandoned for want of provisions. Ali was on this occasion standard-bearer, and was presented with a new banner, the famous Black Eagle, which had been made out of a mantle belonging to Ayesha, the Prophet's wife. He distinguished himself by many brave deeds, and wonderful stories are told of his prodigious strength. Once when he had lost his shield Ali tore down part of a doorway and used the large piece of timber as a shield.

Though the Jews held out well for a time, they were at last overpowered, and one by one the garrisons of the different forts surrendered. The rich vale of Khaibar was added to the territory of the Moslems, but the Jews were allowed to remain in possession of their lands on condition of paying a yearly tribute.

While at Khaibar, the Prophet narrowly escaped being poisoned. A dish of roast kid was placed before him by a Jewess, and as soon as he had swallowed the first mouthful he suspected that the meat was poisoned. One of his companions who had eaten more of the dish died in a very short time, and Mohammed never quite got over the effects of the poison to the end of his life.

The time was now approaching for the fulfilment of the agreement in the Treaty of Peace, allowing the Moslems to visit Meccah. After seven long years the exiles were again to see their native place and worship at the holy shrine. Two thousand pilgrims left Medinah with the Prophet at their head. Some were mounted on camels and many went on foot; they were unarmed except for their sheathed swords, which all pilgrims were allowed to carry. As the procession approached Meccah, the inhabitants, according to their agreement, left the city and camped on the surrounding hills. So when the Moslems entered their old home it was silent and deserted as a city of the dead. No one was to be seen in the streets, the houses were closed and empty—no inquisitive eyes peeped through the small loophole windows to see who went by.

An Eastern town is usually a very noisy place, crowds of people fill the narrow streets to over-flowing; there are water-carriers with their large goatskin bags of water, sweetmeat and grain sellers uttering their own peculiar cries to call attention to their wares, beggars asking alms of the passers-by, children at play, and sometimes camels and donkeys carrying enormous loads of firewood will come pushing through the crowd, upsetting anything that comes in their way. Everywhere there is ceaseless movement and noise, and one is reminded of the restless life and constant buzz in a hive of bees. After the quiet of a Western country town, an Eastern city would strike you as a place of indescribable clamour and confusion.

How strange then for the pilgrims to enter a deserted city, the sound of their footsteps echoing in the empty spaces! Many of the Refugees must have passed by the houses in which they had lived years gone by, before they fled from persecution to join the Prophet at Medinah. One wonders what thoughts filled the mind of Mohammed as, mounted on Al-Kaswa, he rode into the Holy City at the head of two thousand devoted followers. How much had happened since he and Abu Bakr hid in the cave on Mount Thaur and stole silently away under cover of the darkness like hunted animals! Seven years of hard struggle had followed the Flight. Much had been accomplished, but there was still work to be done before idolatry would cease to exist and the worship of the True God be established.

As the pilgrims approached the Kaabah, they called aloud the pilgrim cry, "Labbayk, Labbayk!" which means, "Here am I, at Thy service, O Lord!" Mohammed, still mounted on his camel, went seven times round the sacred building, touching the Black Stone with his staff as he passed. This circling of the Kaabah was a very ancient ceremony, practised by the pilgrims many years before the time of Mohammed. The next place of visitation was the little hill of Safa; seven times the pilgrims walked hurriedly between this hill and the hill of Marwah, in remembrance of Hagar, who, according to Arab tradition, had run distractedly between these two hills in search of water for her son Ishmael. To this day the same rite is practised by all pilgrims who visit Meccah. At every place of visitation prayers were offered up, and after the sacrifice of the victims the ceremonies ended.

The next day a strange scene took place. The Moslem call to prayer, "Allah hu Akbar," "God is great," sounded over the idolatrous city, as Bilal, standing on the roof of the Kaabah, summoned the Faithful to the midday prayers. In answer to the well-known call the Moslems assembled in the open space before the Holy Temple, and the Prophet led the prayers exactly as he was accustomed to do in the mosque at Medinah.

Thus was the True God again worshipped at the Kaabah, which had been for so long the temple of idolatry. Around the worshippers stood the strange figures of the three hundred and sixty idols of Meccah. Some were but rude masses of unhewn stone, one was in the form of a horse, another of an eagle, and among the chief was the giant figure of Hubal, holding in his hand the headless arrows.

The steep mount of Abu Kubais almost over-hangs the eastern side of Meccah, and its summit commands a fine view of the city and the Kaabah. Many of the Meccans were assembled on this mountain top, and looked down with curious eyes on the Moslem worshippers below. There must have been some who were impressed by what they saw, for several conversions followed Mohammed's departure from Meccah.

You will not have forgotten Khalid, the brave Meccan leader who defeated the Moslems at Uhud, and on many occasions distinguished himself by his reckless daring. Khalid could not bear the humiliation of seeing the Prophet enter Meccah, so he had left the city before the arrival of the pilgrims. But not long was he to continue hostile to the Faith of Islam. Khalid had a brother who had been converted soon after the battle of Badr, and it is supposed that he was influenced by his brother's persuasions. For, shortly after the Prophet's pilgrimage, Khalid set out to journey to Medinah, having resolved to make his submission to Islam and embrace the Faith he had opposed and persecuted. On the way he fell in with Amr, another renowned warrior, afterwards famous as the conqueror of Egypt. He too was travelling to the city of the Prophet to give allegiance to the new Faith. Another important convert was Othman, son of the Meccan standard-bearer who was killed at Uhud.

The Taking of Meccah

When the Prophet summoned the nations of the earth to join the Faith of Islam, one of his letters was addressed to the Governor of Ghassan, a dependency of the Roman Empire on the borders of Syria. The messenger carrying this letter was murdered at a place called Mutah. To avenge his death, Mohammed sent an army of three thousand men under the command of Zaid. You will remember the history of this Zaid, who had once been the Prophet's slave, but had afterwards been freed and adopted as a son.

The Moslems little knew what they were undertaking; when they reached the Syrian border they were confronted by an army such as they had never dreamed of, and for the first time had to face the Roman phalanx. The two armies met at Mutah, the very place where the messenger had been murdered. Accustomed to the warfare of desert tribes, it was impossible for the Moslem army to contend with any chance of success against the trained legions of the Roman Empire. Nevertheless, Zaid led his troops against this overwhelming force. He was soon struck down by the enemy's spears, and the command was taken by Ali's brother, Jafar. Though many times wounded, Jafar fought valiantly until he was stabbed by a Roman soldier. A third leader took his place, but he too fell, and the day was lost. The enemy broke through the ranks of the Moslems, who would have been utterly destroyed had not another brave leader succeeded in rallying the scattered remnants of the army and making an orderly retreat. It was Khalid, fighting for the first time on the Moslem side, who thus saved the day from being yet more disastrous. Many a time after this was Khalid to lead the Moslems to battle, winning for himself the title of the "Sword of God." Fierce and relentless, he was often reproved by the Prophet for his harsh acts, yet no man ever possessed a more generous nature than this fiery son of the desert. For Mohammed he had the deepest reverence, and when in battle, always wore a lock of the Prophet's hair fastened to his helmet.

There was sorrow and wailing in Medinah on the return of the ill-fated expedition. Mohammed was deeply grieved at the loss of his two friends; entering the house of his cousin Jafar, he tenderly embraced the fatherless children, and their mother guessed the news he brought. He ordered food to be sent to Jafar's house. "No food will be prepared there to-day," he said, "for all are overwhelmed with grief for the loss of their master." The Prophet next went to Zaid's house, where he was met by Zaid's little daughter, who threw herself weeping into his arms, and Mohammed wept until he sobbed aloud, for her father had been his beloved friend for many years. Though the Prophet could be stern and pitiless to his enemies, he had a very tender heart, and it is said that he always won the affection of children and animals.

After the battle of Mutah there was great unrest among the Arab tribes on the Syrian border, who even threatened to attack Medinah. A second army was sent to wipe out the defeat of Mutah; though no great battle was fought, the expedition met with success, and Amr, who was in command, received the allegiance of several of the border tribes.

When the Treaty of Peace was made at Hudaibiyah, it was agreed that for the space of ten years war should cease between the Meccans and the Moslems. For two years the agreement had not been broken, when the Banu Bakr, a tribe allied to the Meccans, attacked the men of a Moslem tribe, and killed several of them. Some of the chief men of the Kuraysh had disguised themselves and assisted their allies. Thereupon forty men of the tribe who had been thus wrongfully attacked mounted their camels and rode in haste to Medinah. They complained to the Prophet of the breaking of the Treaty, and besought him to punish the offenders. Mohammed promised that he would see the injured men righted, and avenge the murders.

Abu Sufyan, alarmed at the possible consequences of having broken faith with Mohammed, went himself to Medinah to try to make peace. The Prophet would make no promises, and Abu Sufyan begged Omar to intercede for him, but he indignantly refused. Ali and Fatimah were then asked to persuade the Prophet to renew the terms of peace, but all to no purpose. Some time before this Mohammed had married a widowed daughter of Abu Sufyan. On his arrival in Medinah Abu Sufyan paid a visit to his daughter, and was about to seat himself on a mat when she hastily drew it away, saying that no idolater should touch the Prophet's carpet. The chief of the Kuraysh does not seem to have had a very cordial reception in Medinah! Unable to come to any terms with Mohammed, he departed, ill-satisfied with the results of his mission.

Soon after these events, great preparations for some warlike undertaking were going on in Medinah. All was bustle and stir, arms were sharpened and armour put in order, but as yet no one had been told against whom he was to fight! Even Abu Bakr, Mohammed's closest friend and adviser, was kept in ignorance, and Ayesha, as she prepared the Prophet's armour, had still no idea in what direction the army was to march. None knew until the last moment that the Prophet had planned an attack upon Meccah!

So well was the secret guarded that the Meccans had no warning of the vast army that was marching down upon them until they saw ten thousand watch-fires blazing from the mountain tops. The Prophet had ordered every man to kindle a fire, in the hope that the Meccans, overawed by the great display, would at once realize the uselessness of resisting so mighty a force, for Mohammed was anxious to avoid shedding the blood of his countrymen.

Terror and dismay spread through Meccah on this unlooked-for alarm. The day had closed peacefully over the doomed city, and now in the darkness of night the inhabitants were suddenly aware of a mighty army, encamped on the heights overlooking the town.

Abu Sufyan, with a few companions, hurried out on to the Medinah road; the night was very dark, and the mountain tops seemed on fire with the brilliant blaze. Suddenly a voice was heard in the darkness, calling Abu Sufyan by name: "Mohammed is encamped with an army of ten thousand strong! Make thy peace with him and throw in thy lot with Islam." The speaker was Abbas, the Prophet's uncle. Though always on friendly terms with his nephew, he could never make up his mind to acknowledge him as a Prophet until he saw that there was no withstanding him. Now, late in the day, he had joined the winning side, and he begged Abu Sufyan to accompany him to the Moslem camp.

Perhaps Abu Sufyan felt that further resistance was useless, and acknowledged himself defeated in the long struggle with his opponent; perhaps he was convinced that the God who had helped Mohammed to overcome his enemies in the face of so much opposition was, indeed, the True God; whatever may have been his thoughts, he followed Abbas to the tent of the Prophet.

The next morning, the proud Abu Sufyan, chief of the Kuraysh, made his profession of the Faith of Islam, acknowledging the once despised exile to be the Apostle of God. Mohammed received the submission of his enemy graciously, and bade him return to Meccah and tell the people that none should be harmed who offered no resistance and took refuge in their houses or in the Holy Temple. The army was about to march as Abu Sufyan took his leave. He was amazed at the order and discipline of that great host. "Truly," he said to Abbas as he watched the troops of the desert file by, "thy nephew is ruler of a great kingdom!" "He is more than a king," replied Abbas, "for he is a mighty Prophet:" Abu Sufyan hastened back to Meccah to deliver Mohammed's message.

The army marched in four divisions. Each was to enter the city by a different road, and the commanders were given strict orders not to fight unless first attacked. The road followed by the Prophet passed close to the cemetery where Khadijah and Abu Talib lay buried. No army came out to oppose the Moslems as they approached the city, and Mohammed offered up a prayer of thankfulness, for his heart yearned to be at peace with his countrymen.

The only column which met with any opposition was that led by Khalid. Some of the Prophet's bitterest enemies, refusing to be reconciled to him, had posted themselves on a mountain ridge above the town, where they intended to make a last stand. They assailed Khalid and his Bedouins with a shower of arrows, but, after a short skirmish, were put to flight; a few were killed on both sides. The Prophet was much grieved that any bloodshed should have taken place, but, with the exception of this encounter, Meccah surrendered peaceably, acknowledging the supremacy of Mohammed.

On entering the Holy City, Mohammed went to the Kaabah, making the seven circuits of the sacred building. And now followed one of the supreme moments of the Prophet's life. The time had come for the downfall of the idols of Meccah! Mohammed, who had once suffered persecution and exile for condemning the worship of these same idols, now ordered their destruction, and on this, his day of victory, the Meccans dared not raise a finger to save the gods of their fathers. "Truth is come," exclaimed the Prophet, "and falsehood is fled away: verily falsehood is a fleeting thing."

Pointing with his staff to the giant figure of Hubal, he ordered it to be destroyed; it was hewn in pieces and fell with a crash to the ground. One by one, these guardian gods of the city were singled out for destruction, until, of the three hundred and sixty, not one remained standing. On the walls of the Kaabah were pictures of Abraham and the angels; these were effaced by Omar, who rubbed them out with a cloth, for the Moslems consider pictures, as well as images, symbols of idolatry. "Thou shalt not make to thyself any graven image, nor the likeness of anything that is in heaven above or in the earth beneath, or in the water under the earth." This commandment is obeyed literally by the followers of the Prophet.

Thus was idolatry rooted out of Meccah, and henceforth the national shrine of Arabia was to be the Temple of the True God.

From that great day of Mohammed's final victory to the present time, the Moslem call to prayer has daily been heard from the Kaabah of Meccah, and public prayer has been performed in the same words as those used by the Prophet.

After the destruction of the idols, Mohammed preached to the assembled people. "Sons of the Kuraysh, how think you that I should deal with you?" he asked, when he had finished his discourse. "With kindness and mercy, gracious brother," they replied. The Prophet, deeply moved, said he would act towards his kinsmen even as Joseph had acted towards his brethren. "I shall not reproach you," he said; "God will forgive, He is merciful and compassionate."

Mohammed won the hearts of his countrymen by the generosity he showed the vanquished city. Meccah, which had cast him forth an exile and an outlaw, was now at his mercy, but all thoughts of revenge were laid aside, and Mohammed freely forgave his enemies except a few persons who were guilty of various crimes, and of these only two were condemned to death.

So great a love did the Prophet cherish for his native city that he declared it to be the fairest spot on earth, and the men of Medinah feared he would desert them and make Meccah his home. But he assured the Helpers that he would never forsake them, for had they not given him a home in his exile, and made him welcome when all the rest of the world was against him! "Where ye live I shall live," he said, "and there too shall I die."

In the evening, when the Prophet had retired to his tent, Abu Bakr brought his father to see him. Abu Kuhafah, blind and bowed with age, with hair "white as the flower of the mountain grass," was led into the Prophet's presence. Mohammed received the old man kindly and bade him sit down beside him. "Thy father should have stayed in his own house," he said to Abu Bakr, "and I would have gone to see him there." Abu Kuhafah was easily persuaded to join the Faith of which his son was such a devoted follower. He lived to be ninety-seven, and to see Abu Bakr elected Khalif, or successor of the Prophet.

During the days following Mohammed's entry into Meccah, great numbers of the inhabitants came to him to take the oath of allegiance, and make their profession of the Faith of Islam. On these occasions every man placed his hand on that of the Prophet, in token of his oath, repeating the words of the Second or Great Pledge of Al-Akabah. The women stepped forward and pledged themselves in the words of the "Women's Pledge" (or "First Pledge of Al Akabah ") to worship none but the True God, to lead pure and virtuous lives, and obey the Prophet in all that was right. Mohammed would then say, "Go, for you have pledged yourselves"—he did not take the women by the hand.

You must not suppose that all the inhabitants of Meccah were converted at once; none were urged to pledge themselves until they had studied the new religion. There were no doubt some who joined because they wished to be on the winning side, but the doctrines of Islam had been slowly gaining ground during the eight years since the Flight, and many were prepared to receive them. The great aim of the Prophet's life had been accomplished, idolatry was overthrown, and the standard of the Faith had been planted in the Holy City.

The Submission of Taif

During the time that Mohammed was in Meccah, he ordered the destruction of several shrines of idolatry in the neighbourhood. Khalid, with a party of armed men, overthrew the temple of a famous Meccan goddess in the valley of Nakhla, and other chiefs were sent out to destroy the idols of some of the tribes who had become Moslems. The people of Taif (the city in which Mohammed had once tried to plant the Faith) began to fear for their great image, Al-Lat, for which they had a special devotion. Determined to strike a blow for their ancient religion, they called all their allies to their help, and the combined forces assembled in great numbers near the valley of Hunain, between Meccah and Taif.

The Prophet had arrived in Meccah at the head of ten thousand men. To these were now added two thousand newly-converted Meccans, so the army which marched out to meet the men of Taif and their allies numbered twelve thousand. But this imposing army came very near to being defeated. The Thakifites (as the people of Taif were called) concealed themselves among the rough rocks overlooking a steep and narrow pass at the entrance to the valley of Hunain. There, they waited in silence until they saw the Moslems enter the pass, when they rushed headlong upon them, taking them completely by surprise. The suddenness of the attack in the uncertain light of dawn produced a panic among the Moslem troops, cramped in the narrow space between the steep walls of the mountain. They fled in disorder down the pass, and the camels, taking fright, were jammed across the narrow gorge. All was confusion and clamour, and few heeded the voice of the Prophet, calling on his men to rally. Among those who stood by him were Abbas, Ali, Omar and Abu Bakr. Abbas, who had a powerful voice, cried aloud, "Ye citizens of Medinah, ye men of the Pledge of the Tree!" This call, repeated again and again, reached the ears of the fugitives and brought to their minds the oath they had sworn, to defend the Prophet with their lives. A hundred of his devoted disciples fought their way to his side, others followed their example, and by degrees the whole army rallied and faced the enemy. The fighting was very severe, but in the end the Moslems triumphed; the men of Taif fled and were pursued with great slaughter. The whole of the enemy's camp, containing all the women and children, fell into the hands of the Moslems, who captured six thousand prisoners and much spoil, including twenty-four thousand camels and forty thousand sheep and goats. The prisoners and the spoil were sent to the valley of Ji'irranah to await distribution.

Meanwhile, the Prophet led his army on to Taif, and laid siege to the city. It was very strongly fortified, and there was no lack of water and provisions within the walls. The defenders were skilled archers, and the showers of arrows, with which they assailed the Moslems, darkened the sky like clouds of locusts. When an attempt was made to undermine the walls, the citizens flung down balls of red-hot iron from the battlements. Finding he could make no impression on the besieged city, Mohammed, as a last resource, ordered the beautiful vineyards surrounding the city of Taif to be cut down. But the inhabitants sent him such an earnest appeal to spare their vineyards, "for the sake of mercy and of God," that he relented, and stopped the work of destruction. The Moslems were encamped about a month before Taif, but the city showed no signs of surrender, so Mohammed withdrew his army and abandoned the siege.

From Taif, the Moslems marched to the valley of Ji'irranah, where the prisoners and the spoil taken in the battle of Hunain had been sent. Some of the prisoners had known the Prophet when, as a child, he had lived in the tents of a wandering desert tribe, and among the women was one who claimed to be his foster-sister. Her name was Al-Shaima, or "the woman with a mark," for she had a mark on her shoulder which she declared had been made by Mohammed when he had once bitten her as she carried him on her hip. The Prophet recognized the little girl who had played with him and carried him about as a young child, and he talked affectionately to her of those early days. She was at once re-leased and sent back to her kindred with a handsome present.

Seeing his kindness to his old playmate, the prisoners sent a petition

to the Prophet, begging that they might be set free. "We have known thee as a little child," they said, "then as a noble youth and now that thou hast attained to such power and dignity be merciful to us." Mohammed could not resist this touching appeal, and generously consented to release all the prisoners.

The flocks and herds and various spoil were now distributed among the soldiers. Mohammed gave handsome presents to the chiefs of Meccah, some of whom received as many as a hundred camels apiece. So liberal was he to his old enemies that the men of Medinah felt themselves slighted, and said one to another, "He has joined his own people and has forsaken us." Mohammed was grieved when he heard of these murmurings among his faithful followers. "Ye Helpers," he said to them, "why are ye disturbed because I have sought to gain over the hearts of these men? Are ye not satisfied that they should have the flocks and herds, while ye have the Prophet of the Lord with you? I will never leave you—if all men were to go one way, and the men of Medinah another, I would follow the men of Medinah. The Lord bless them and their sons for ever." The people were touched at the words of the Prophet, and many wept, while they cried out with one voice, "We are well satisfied, O Prophet!" Soon after these events Mohammed, having appointed a governor over Meccah, led his army back to Medinah.

As the conqueror of Meccah, Mohammed was acknowledged to be the chief ruler in Arabia, and many tribes, even in the most distant parts of the peninsula, sent deputations to make their submission. Envoys travelled from Yemen in the south, Oman on the Persian Gulf, from the borders of Syria and Persia, to make treaties with the great chief whose fame had already spread afar. For Mohammed had founded, not a religion only, but an empire; in uniting the scattered desert tribes by the ties of a common faith he made of them a nation, and laid the foundation of the great Saracen empire, which was to play so great a part in the world's history.

The envoys who came to Medinah were received in the courtyard of the mosque, which served as hall of audience, and was the place where all affairs of state were discussed. Though Mohammed had attained to so much power, he continued to live the simple life of an Arab. The humble row of dwellings which he had built for his wives along the eastern side of the mosque served him for a palace, while his crown was the turban worn by his ancestors. But though he had neither crown nor palace, no man was ever more a king in the hearts of his people. Omar, thinking that the Prophet should be royally adorned when receiving deputations, suggested that he should buy a silk robe to wear on these occasions, but Mohammed refused to make any change in his habits. The simplicity of the Prophet's mode of life is a great contrast to the luxury and splendour of some of the later Khalifs.

The greater number of the tribes of Arabia had now acknowledged the supremacy of Mohammed; some of these had been converted to Islam, and others had made treaties agreeing to pay tribute to the Apostle of God. So many deputations were sent to Medinah during the ninth year since the Flight, that this year came to be called the "Year of Deputations." The city of Taif was one of the few that still held aloof.

Shortly after Mohammed's return to Medinah, a chief of Taif, named Urwah, had come to visit the Prophet to inquire into the doctrines of Islam. He retuned to his city a Moslem, and determined to convince his countrymen of their error in persisting in the worship of idols. The people of Taif, obstinate as ever in their devotion to Al-Lat, fell upon Urwah and stoned him; and he died thanking God for the honour of martyrdom. Whether through remorse at having slain Urwah, or because they suffered from the opposition of neighbouring tribes, who were now all believers, the Thakifites decided to enter into an agreement with Mohammed. They therefore sent six of their chief men to Medinah to arrange a treaty. The Prophet had just returned from an expedition to Syria when the envoys from Taif arrived. Having heard rumours of a Roman invasion, Mohammed had led a large army to Tabuk, a town near the Syrian border; but the rumour proved to be false, and the army returned to Medinah, having suffered much through the heat and want of water. This was the last campaign undertaken by the Prophet.

The chiefs of Taif were kindly received by Mohammed, who pitched a tent for them just outside the mosque, and in the evenings, after supper, he used to go and sit with them to discuss their affairs. He was not long in convincing them of the truth of the doctrines of Islam; but though the six chiefs believed, the people of Taif, they said, would never consent to the destruction of their great idol. Mohammed replied that the worship of the True God could not exist side by side with the worship of idols, and that if the people of Taif wished to join his standard Al-Lat must be destroyed at once. The chiefs begged that the idol might at any rate remain standing for three years, during which time the people could be instructed in the new faith; but Mohammed would not consent to this. The chiefs then pleaded that two years might be allowed to pass before the destruction of the idol, but this request was also refused. "Then give us one year," they said; "six months—one month"; but Mohammed would make no compromise. Seeing that the Prophet was firmly resolved, the chiefs of Taif agreed, though unwillingly, to have the great idol destroyed without delay. They next begged that the Thakifites might be excused the five daily prayers and the frequent washings, for they feared the people would find these observances a burden. Mohammed said that there could be no true religion without prayer, and that the people of Taif must do as the other Moslems did. One more request the chiefs made before taking their departure, and that was that they should not be obliged to destroy the image with their own hands. So Abu Sufyan and Mughirah, a nephew of the martyr Urwah, were sent with them to overthrow the great goddess of Taif.

A strange scene took place on the return of the chiefs to their native city. Mughirah, carrying a pick-axe, and surrounded by a guard of armed men, made his way to the temple of the goddess. The people had assembled in great numbers, and the women uttered loud lamentations, fearing that some terrible catastrophe would follow the overthrow of Al-Lat. All held their breath in anxious suspense as the first stroke of the axe descended upon the figure of the goddess. Before long the image was hacked in pieces, and the people looked on the scattered fragments of the object of their worship.

Thus did Taif at length make her submission. This city had been one of the greatest strongholds of idolatry, and the people gave their allegiance to Islam unwillingly, and more from reasons of state than from religious motives. As time passed, however, the memory of the old gods faded, and "falsehood fled away; verily falsehood is a fleeting thing."

The Farewell Pilgrimage

The four great duties which every good Moslem is expected to perform are Prayer, Almsgiving, Fasting, and Pilgrimage. Every follower of the Prophet, having the necessary health and means, should go, at least once in his life, as a pilgrim to Meccah. The full ceremonies of the "Greater Pilgrimage" can only be performed in the sacred month of Dhul Hijjah, the "Lesser Pilgrimage," consisting of fewer ceremonies, can be made at any other time of the year.

The practice of going to Meccah on pilgrimage was a very ancient one, as I have already told you, and I think the Prophet's chief reason for continuing it was that he realized the great power and strength of unity. At Meccah, Moslems of all nations meet together; from the plains of India, the snowy fastnesses of Afghanistan and Baltistan, from Persia, Syria, Turkey and Asia Minor, from Egypt and various parts of Africa to the shores of the Atlantic, the stream of pilgrims flows toward the central shrine of the Faith, the "Bayt Allah," or House of God. This is the name commonly used by Moslems for the Kaabah, and it is the same name as the Hebrew "Beth-el," which means House of God.

In the ninth year of Islam Abu Bakr led about three hundred pilgrims to Meccah for the "Greater Pilgrimage." There were, of course, still a good many idolaters in different parts of Arabia, and these came, as usual, to Meccah in the pilgrimage season. Many of the ceremonies they practised were degraded and idolatrous, and the Prophet determined that henceforward none but the worship of the True God should be celebrated at the holy shrine. He therefore sent Ali with a proclamation, to be read to the assembled pilgrims, ordering that in future no idolater should enter the sacred territory of Meccah.

In the following year Mohammed led a vast multitude of pilgrims to the Holy City. This great pilgrimage of the Prophet has been taken as a model for all succeeding ones, and exactly as he performed the ceremonies on this occasion, so have his followers performed them to the present day. The rites of the Greater Pilgrimage occupy three days, and include a visit to Mount Arafat, also called the Mount of Mercy, a sacred hill about twelve miles east of Meccah. Between Arafat and Meccah lies the valley of Mina, a sandy valley surrounded by low hills. There, Mohammed, and the many thousand pilgrims who followed him, en-camped on the opening day of the Great Pilgrimage. At dawn the next morning, after the early prayers, the Prophet mounted his camel and continued his way to Arafat. Al-Kaswa, who had carried her master to safety when he fled from Meccah, carried him now, on the memorable occasion of his last pilgrimage. Arafat is a rough granite hill, about two hundred feet high, standing alone on the sandy plain; upon its summit is a spot called "Adam's place of prayer," which is connected with an old legend. The day at Arafat was spent in prayer and religious obser-vance. After dusk, Mohammed mounted Al-Kaswa and sped hurriedly in the moonlight to a place on the road to Mina, called Muzdalifah, where he passed the night. In every particular is the Prophet's example followed by the pilgrims of the present day, who always leave Arafat in haste and confusion, and proceed at headlong speed to Muzdalifah, accidents often happening on the way.

The following day, on the pilgrims' return to Mina, a strange ceremo-ny took place, called the "Stoning of the Devil." A tradition tells that Abraham, crossing the valley of Mina, once met the Devil and drove him away by stoning him; to commemorate this event every pilgrim throws a number of small stones at certain rocky projections along the Mina Valley. Thus the ceremonies of pilgrimage are a curious mixture of acts of true devotion and strange rites connected with ancient leg-ends and traditions. The closing ceremony is the sacrifice of the victims, which takes place at Mina, on the third day of pilgrimage. This sacrifice is an old pagan custom, which survived along with other ancient rites, for in reality sacrifice plays no part in the religion of Islam as instituted by Mohammed.

The Prophet's mission was now fulfilled, his work was done; for had he not overthrown idolatry and established the worship of One God in all parts of Arabia! This was the aim which he had set himself in those early days of doubt and struggle in the solitudes of Mount Hira, and he was not one to look back when he had once put his hand to the plough. His life's labour had been nobly accomplished. It seems that on this, his last visit to Meccah, Mohammed already felt that his end was approaching, and before leaving Mina (after the completion of the Pilgrimage) he addressed his followers in words which remained long in their memories.

The sun was declining, and the grey hills flamed into sudden splendour, as the Prophet, seated on Al-Kaswa, gathered his people round him. "Ye people," he began, "listen to my words; for I know not whether after this year I shall ever be amongst you here again." He then exhorted his followers to observe the commands he had given them, to beware the temptations of Satan and the sin of idolatry. He enjoined them to treat their wives kindly, and to respect life and property. "And your slaves," continued the Prophet, "see that ye feed them with such food as ye eat yourselves, and clothe them with the stuff ye wear. They are the servants of the Lord and are not to be tormented." The Prophet impressed on his followers the doctrine of the brotherhood of Islam. "Ye people," he said, "hearken to my speech and understand the same. Know that every Moslem is the brother of every other Moslem. All of you are on the same equality. Ye are one Brotherhood."

When he had finished his discourse the Prophet raised his hands to heaven and cried, "Lord, I have delivered my message and fulfilled my mission!" And the people replied as with one voice: "Yea, truly hast thou done so!" The assembly was then dismissed. On his return to Meccah, Mohammed entered the Kaabah and prayed within its walls. He remained for three days in Meccah and then went back to Medinah.

Though the Prophet seemed to feel that his life was drawing to a close, he appeared to be in his ordinary health, and attended to his business as usual. Abu Bakr, however, must have noticed signs of advancing age in his beloved master, for he one day exclaimed sorrowfully, "Alas! grey hairs are hastening upon thee!" Mohammed was then sixty-three years old.

Not many months after his return from the Great Pilgrimage the

DISCOVERY
PUBLISHER

Prophet was attacked by a fever. For some days he struggled against the disease and went, as usual, into the mosque to lead the prayers. At length, however, he was forced to give in, and retired to the house of Ayesha, by whom he was tenderly nursed during his illness. He ordered Abu Bakr to lead the prayers in his absence.

The courtyard of the mosque was now hushed and quiet; the people only entered it during the hours of prayer, or when they came to make anxious inquiries after the Prophet's health. Mohammed suffered great pain and weakness and for several days was in a high fever. One day, calling Ayesha to his side, he asked her for some gold which he had given her to take care of; on her bringing the money he ordered it all to be distributed among the poor. "It would not have become me," he said, "to meet my Lord with this gold in my possession."

At the end of a few days the fever was less violent and Mohammed seemed a little stronger. Many people, hearing of his sickness, came from afar to inquire after him, and during the hours of prayer the mosque was often crowded with worshippers. One day as Abu Bakr was leading the midday prayers, the curtain of Ayesha's doorway was softly pushed aside, and the Prophet himself entered the mosque. All those who saw him enter noticed the peaceful and radiant smile which lit up his face. Perhaps, as he gazed on the assembly of earnest and devout Believers, he felt that his work was finished, and he might now take his rest. Leaning on the arm of his cousin, one of the sons of Abbas, Mohammed walked slowly to the side of Abu Bakr and seated himself on the ground near him. When the prayers were ended, the Prophet talked with several of his friends, who were rejoiced to see him, as they thought, so much better. Seated in the courtyard of the mosque, he then spoke a few words to the people, but these exertions were too much for him and he returned to Ayesha's house very exhausted. Tenderly, Ayesha supported her husband's drooping head and rubbed his cold hands, while she repeated a prayer she had often heard him use at the bedside of sick people. "Take away evil and misfortune, O thou Lord of mankind! Grant a cure, for Thou art the best Physician." It was but two hours after his return from the mosque that Mohammed peace-

fully breathed his last.

A legend tells that Gabriel, descending for the last time to earth, came to visit the dying Prophet; with him was another angel, the Angel of Death, who stood without asking permission to enter. When Mohammed gave him leave, the Angel of Death entered the house and, standing before the Prophet, asked him if he should take his soul or leave it? Never before had mortal man been given this choice. "Do even as thou art commanded," said Mohammed, signifying his readiness to meet his Lord. And Gabriel uttered the last blessing, "Peace be upon thee, O Apostle of God," as the soul of Mohammed passed away.

When it was known that the Prophet was dead, the people were seized with dismay and knew not what to make of it. So lately had they seen and spoken with him that many refused to believe that he had been taken from them. Some seem to have thought that he would never die, and the news came as a terrible shock. Omar, overcome with grief, was quite unable to face the bitter truth. "He is not dead," he cried, "he has only swooned, and will return to us—he has gone to his Lord, as Moses did when he was absent forty days." Drawing his sword, Omar spoke wildly and excitedly to the people in the mosque, threatening anyone who dared to say that the Prophet was dead.

Suddenly, a stern voice commanded silence, and Abu Bakr addressed the people in calm and reasonable words. Mohammed had always told them, he said, that he was but a man like themselves, and would die as other men died. "If he were to die, would ye turn back from your faith," said Abu Bakr, quoting the words of the Koran. "Do ye worship Mohammed! Then know that he indeed is dead, but the God of Mohammed liveth and can never die!"

MOHAMMED PREACHING HIS FAREWELL SERMON

www.ingramcontent.com/pod-product-compliance
Lightning Source LLC
LaVergne TN
LVHW091155080426
835509LV00006B/689